The
SATNAMI
STORY

Special Notice

Plans are underway to publish a three- to four-volume biography of Donald McGavran by Vern Middleton. The first volume will be published late in 1990 and the others will follow. If you wish to be informed when these are available, please send your name and address to

McGavran Biography
William Carey Library
P.O. Box 40129
Pasadena, CA   91114

The
SATNAMI
STORY

A Thrilling Drama of
Religious Change

Donald A. McGavran

William Carey Library

PASADENA, CALIFORNIA

Published by
William Carey Library
P.O. Box 40129
Pasadena, CA   91114
(818) 798-0819

ISBN 0-87808-225-5

**Library of Congress Cataloging-in-Publication
Data**

McGavran, Donald Anderson, 1897-1990

The Satnami story: a thrilling drama of
religious change / by Donald McGavran.
p.   cm.
ISBN 0-87808-225-5 :
1. Missions to Satnamis--History--20th century.
2. Missions--India--History--20th century.
3. India--Church history--20th century.
4. McGavran, Donald Anderson
I. Title.
BV2628.S37M42   1989
266'.00954'0904--dc20   89-39652
                                                   CIP

Contents

Contents

Foreword

Dutch missiologist J. Verkuyl[1] notes the powerful influence of church growth theory on the contemporary mission scene, both among evangelicals and non-evangelicals. The dean of Dutch missiologists devotes several pages to the role of Donald McGavran, father of the church growth movement. The world of mission studies knows McGavran the researcher, strategist, and apologist for the Christian world mission.

In *The Satnami Story, A Drama of Religious Change*, we meet McGavran the field missionary. The autobiographical content makes it a delightful narrative which also provides glimpses of missionary life and labour in mid-India in the mid-twentieth century. Here we meet McGavran the church planter!

McGavran, who was born in India of missionary parents, a third generation missionary, started his work in India for six years as an educator. He spent the next three years as the secretary-treasurer for his mission of 70 missionaries. He then went on for the next 18 years of his work in India as an evangelist. Church growth theory evolved from the crucible of field experience during these 18 years, 1936-1954.

Critics of the church growth movement sometimes have objected to what some regard as an excessive emphasis on pragmatism to the neglect of theology. What they fail to discern is that the very platform from which McGavran began his polemic was a positive protest grounded in a very basic theology.

If McGavran appears quite hospitable toward a wide range of theological options embracing a vast array of doctrinal emphases and denominational differences, that generosity ought not be misconstrued as theological indifference or carelessness. Tolerant, yes, and willing to leave the intricacies of theological debate to the experts, McGavran's position is quite doctrinaire: *the direct command of God and the lostness of mankind demand that the good news of Christ be proclaimed in all the world among all peoples to the end that they be persuaded to repentance, faith, and lifelong discipleship, to serve God in the fellowship of Christ's Church.*

It is not true that McGavran's central emphasis is numerical increase in numbers of churches and members as Taber[2] for example, suggests. For McGavran the central theological and pragmatic issue is discipling the *ethne* of the world—*jatiyan*, castes, tribes, clans, neighbourhoods. From this central concern flow various other considerations, practical and methodological as well as theological.

McGavran cannot be fully understood apart from the experience of India. *The Satnami Story* gets us into the realities of the struggle to communicate the gospel in an indifferent and sometimes hostile non-Christian setting. McGavran's critics seem to have little comprehension of what that entails. In fact, as Taber[3] points out, the critics speak to a far different world, i.e., modern "secular" society, which is a very different reality from the 4 or 5 million peasants—often landless—followers of popular Hinduism, among whom McGavran laboured as a frontier missionary and in which his earlier concepts germinated.

Several entertaining anecdotes depict Donald McGavran engaged in the daily routine of running a mission station. McGavran is no arm-chair dreamer. His theories emerge from the hard experience of beginning church growth and the emergence of "mission compound Christianity" in a resistant part of Mid India. The Christian Mission engaged in countless deeds of compassion and service as well as proclamation of the gospel. Out of this experience McGavran relates several stages and steps in church planting.

This point is important. McGavran's Indian critics include on the one hand leaders who do not believe in evangelisation and who unfairly charge that evangelicals spiritualise the gospel and neglect the social dimension. The record shows that social ministries actually accounted for the greatest amount of budget, personnel, and programme. McGavran's was quite a typical case. On the other hand, critics have been Indian evangelicals who apparently fear church growth theory and practice but who themselves have served as neither church planters or crosscultural missionaries in their own country.

McGavran is adamant that evangelisation will not be accomplished by social ministries, nor by Western money in the hands of evangelicals engaged in petty projects and good deeds but making little directed effort toward creating new bands of believers on new ground in every people, every segment of society. The Satnami is one example of such a people. The story which McGavran narrates is the effort in which he engaged, sometimes with success, more often failure, to bring a slightly responsive piece of the human mosaic to Christian faith and discipleship.

Today's world is an exciting arena for evangelisation, particularly in the two-thirds world. Explosive church growth is seen in Africa but also in Asian countries such as Korea. Let this not obscure the fact that at least two-thirds of humanity does not yet name the name of Christ. Countless segments of the human race—tribes and tongues, villagers and urbanites, entire populations—are yet to be confronted with the gospel in a meaningful way. The Satnami is but one such case. Each people is distinctive, every culture unique. The Christian message is to be clearly communicated in every human society whether Hindu or Muslim, Marxist or Buddhist, tribal or urban, atheist or religious, sophisticated or preliterate. McGavran challenges the Indian Church to get on with this central task. The author has devoted most of his life and two careers to bringing the peoples of the world, including those of his beloved India, to faith and obedience.

The narrative which unfolds is descriptive of a people and of missionary life half a century ago. At times the account is explanatory and didactic. Some incidents are raucous and entertaining, e.g., an ill-fated log-floating expedition on a rain-swollen river and a tongue-lashing by an angry village woman. More missionary adventures such as this one should be written to capture events and experiences which otherwise will be lost and forgotten.

The Satnami Story grapples with issues what still confront new believers in Christ in a hostile environment. Economic boycott, when to baptise, problems of nurture, illegal police harassment, how to respond to the problems of poverty and oppression—these are some of the relevant issues which confront the reader. Today's Indian, African, and Latin American missionaries will read with interest how these challenges were faced in a previous generation. But the primary demand of the book is that we consider seriously the evangelisation of every people, tongue, tribe, and caste in the Indian subcontinent and the world.

Roger E. Hedlund
Church Growth Research Centre, Madras, India
1989

References:

1. J. Verkuyl, *Contemporary Missiology*. Eerdmans. 1978.
2. Charles R. Taber, "God vs. Idols: A Model of Conversion." *Journal of the Academy for Evangelism in Theological Education*, Vol. 3, 1987-1988, pp. 20, 23.
3. Ibid.

Preface

No one can sit hour after hour with Dr. McGavran, listening to his accounts and reflections on the world mission enterprise (especially in the context of India), without gaining an invaluable education.

My wife Christy and I had just returned from our third trip to India ministering with the Bethel Agricultural Fellowship and Friends Missionary Prayer Band (two indigenous mission efforts in India). We had been deeply marked by those experiences—the needs, challenges and opportunities facing our brethren in India these days. Dr. Ralph Winter, the general director at the U.S. Center for World Mission, asked if I would be willing to help Dr. McGavran put on paper some of his life and work over the years in India. I was enthusiastic about doing so, especially in response to the growing concern Christy and I had in relationship to India.

I've also had a growing conviction that younger people ought to be learning and helping older more experienced people fulfill some of their dreams and visions as a normal healthy pattern for growing up in our segmented individualistic American society. Not until we have faithfully served the generation ahead of us can we expect to effectively lead the generation behind us. Learning from the generation ahead certainly guards us from assuming we have to go out and reinvent new strategies and processes from scratch. It guards us from falling prey to problems and difficulties that those who've gone before us have already faced and learned a great deal from. We are guarded from fulfilling those familiar words of the Old Testament, "they forgot the ways of their fathers." This project has been one such opportunity to live out this conviction.

Dr. McGavran's age might be telling him that productive, meaningful work is at an end. Yet, because of another Voice, a louder Voice, the Voice of the heavenly Father whose command "make disciples of all nations," rings so loud in his ears, the voice of our culture—"Retire at age 65"—never seems to get through! Dr. McGavran continues to press on. Though his eyes fail and his body gets tired, the life of Christ and His cause still shouts for expression and understanding through him. Assisting in the production of this book has given me the privilege of lending some younger eyes, younger ears, younger feet to Dr. McGavran. In the process, I've heard the resounding command of the Ultimate Authority in the universe a little louder in my own heart and mind: "Disciple all the peoples of the world" (Matthew 28:18-19).

This story takes place among the Satnami peoples of mid-India, where Dr. McGavran and his father before him worked for many years. It illuminates Dr. McGavran's discovery of principles for obeying the Great Commission. Here you'll find the beginnings of the worldwide church growth movement.

The story is a picture of attempting to win a whole *ethnos* (segment of society) to Christ, of starting a people movement. The story is real. It's alive! You can smell the air, hear the sounds, feel the tension. You'll laugh. You'll cry. It's also historical. It's a manual for the education of missionaries, and indeed of all practising Christians. What this book tells us about the evangelisation of the Satnamis in India also relates what is involved in discipling numerous tribes, castes, and clans all over the world. Christ's command to disciple all nations is its central theme. You'll understand its meaning in the context of the peoples of India and of all other countries as well, including North America. Listen carefully. There's something in this book that will stick with you a long time. There's something unchangeable from generation to generation as God carries on His work among all the multitudinous peoples (*ethne*) of the world.

You will note many British spellings of words in this book. After all, India was ruled by the British for 200 years, and this is a story about India.

May this book make a difference in your vision of evangelisation and what an evangelised world might look like. May this book capture our hearts. You cannot read this book without reflecting on our Lord who taught that the good shepherd is always seeking the lost.

Hopefully this book will encourage Christians in their twenties and thirties who are considering missionary work to sit at the feet of those who've gone before them.

Younger missionary candidates ought to have the opportunity to take, for credit, "classes" sitting at the feet of "retired" missionaries helping them put on paper the lessons they have learned. Think what our missions libraries would be filled with if this were happening! May this book be one such in a long series yet to come.

Bruce Graham
U.S. Center for World Mission
1989

1

Let's Leave Idolatry

Ghasi Das shouted, "Throw out your idols. Worship only the true God. Quit eating meat—neither cow meat nor pig meat nor deer meat nor goat meat nor chicken meat. **Eat no meat.** It lowers you in the estimate of the Hindus. Quit keeping chickens, or you'll be tempted to eat them and thus lower the status of our whole caste. Dress in white. Live simply. You're not to eat out of brass vessels or wear brightly coloured clothing. Wait for the coming of a red-faced man with a big hat on his head and a big book in his hand. Do what he tells you."

This was what Ghasi Das shouted to all who would listen. The Chamars asked, "What is the name of the true God whom you proclaim?" Ghasi Das replied, "I don't know, but His is the true name."

Ghasi Das was a Chamar peasant who lived in the early 1800's near the centre of a great plain in the southeast corner of Madhya Pradesh[1] in a village called Bhandar. In 1817 he went on foot on a pilgrimage to the river Ganges, probably to Calcutta. It was 400 miles to the east. The fact that he made such a pilgrimage indicates that he was a man of religious sensitivity. There on the banks of one of the mouths of the Ganges, called the Hoogli, he heard William Carey or some other missionary. He came back with a striking message for the Chamars. It was a challenge, a call to become a new people. Because of their unusual landed nature, his message found immediate and widespread acceptance.

---

[1]A large province in the very centre of India.

Now in Hindi, "true" is *sat* and "name" is *nam*. So "true name" became *sat nam*. Therefore Ghasi Das's followers became the worshippers of Satnam, the True Name. They called themselves True Namers, or Satnamis.

One hundred years later, in 1917, the leaders of the Chungia Chamars, a subcaste of the Chamars that had not become Satnamis, approximately 50,000 souls, called a meeting of their leaders at Set Ganga, where a small brook welled up out of the plain and flowed away to the east. Since water does not ordinarily flow up out of the earth, they believed that some spiritual force was at work. Set Ganga was a holy place.

Hindus had built a small temple there hundreds of years before. As in many other Hindu temples they had placed twelve carved stones around the doorway and on its sides. These depicted naked men and women having sexual intercourse. Set Ganga was a famous place. It was there that the Chungia Chamars decided to hold a great conference in April 1917 after the winter crops had been harvested. There they assembled to consider becoming Christian as a whole people. The Christian evangelist, Hira Lal, was there. The Chungias heard him with rapt attention. Then they said, "You can go now. We'll talk this over amongst ourselves. We have resolved to leave idolatry. Ghasi Das told us to do this a hundred years ago. Just when we leave, however, remains to be decided."

The Hindus, however, had also heard about this gathering of Chungias to decide whether to become Christian. How could the Hindus help but hear this talk among the Chamars, the lowest caste in the plain—in many cases their serfs? To the Hindus, the idea of the Chamars becoming Christians was utterly abhorrent. The Hindus felt they were losing their serfs to the Christians— the white men, who were the rulers of the country. The self-government movement under Gandhi was beginning to get under way. It was not nearly as strong as it would be in a few years, but the Hindi newspapers were talking excitedly about *swaraj* (self-government) in the days when England was fighting for its life against Germany. There was considerable speculation amongst the intelligentsia as to India becoming totally free as soon as Britain was defeated. They did not realise that if Britain was defeated, the Germans would rule India.

Consequently, the Hindu subinspector of police (the highest police officer in that subdistrict) went to Set Ganga. He pitched his tent 200 yards from the Chungia Chamar encampment as he was not going to defile himself by living amongst them. He then summoned the leading Chamars to come to him one by one. He said to each, "Remember, if you become Christian, I'm going to make sure that that case against you where I was lenient is taken up again. If you become Christian, then when other people charge you with offences, I shall do a very thorough investigation. I've been good to you people, but remember that I can be very harsh. Do you understand? If you become Christians, you'll go to jail."

The Chungia Chamars were a timid people. While they had an aristocracy and while a few of them owned large amounts of land, they were, after all, Chamars—Untouchables. They were the victims of the Hindu social order.

To understand the outcome and lessons learned from this absorbing story, readers in India and the Western world must see the background in which it occurred. This will be explained in considerable detail in the following chapters.

A fascinating story will unfold. Read it with care, for the whole process of world evangelisation, so clearly commanded by Christ, is composed of thousands of similar stories, each one differing somewhat from the others.

Readers in Africa, Asia and Latin America will also recognise that effective evangelism now is not accomplished by Christian schools, Christian hospitals, Christian leprosy homes and large amounts of Western money. At present and in the future we shall see a duplication of the New Testament model. Bands of believers will arise which meet in homes, rented halls and occasionally in cemeteries. Exactly as the Communist Party now spreads, exactly as the Church of Jesus Christ spread in the first hundred years of its existence (without erecting buildings), cells of Christian believers will multiply all across India and other lands.

The story of this attempt to disciple a segment of society has some aspects to it which will not be reproduced by Indian pastors, laymen and missionaries as they seek to carry out the Great Commission (*"sab jatiyan ko chela karo"* Matthew 28:19). Each piece of the Indian mosaic will be discipled in a

4 THE SATNAMI STORY

slightly different way. But the central purpose that animates this entire book is now directing all realistic evangelistic efforts in every part of India. Bands of believers will arise in *jati* after *jati* (caste after caste), segment after segment of society. Most of the opportunities and problems recounted in the following pages will face all those who seek to be faithful evangelists of the good news in all parts of the globe.

How shall we define and understand unreached segments of society? In the following pages as the reader sees the Satnami caste being evangelised by five missions and a community of possibly 15,000 Christians, largely of Satnami origin, arising, he may well jump to the conclusion that the Satnami caste was very well reached. Such a conclusion is utterly erroneous. Any segment of society remains unreached until there is within it a Christward movement and its members become followers of the Lord Jesus while still remaining ethnically themselves. As readers in India and America pursue chapter after chapter they will have to guard against the conclusion that the Satnami were, after all, very well evangelised.

An intelligent understanding of the Satnami story will help all readers to form a correct estimate of what evangelism in their particular segment of society really means. If members of the universal Church in all six continents attempt to reach the unreached, if world evangelisation is to be effectively carried out, if eternal God's command (Romans 16:25-26) is to be obeyed, then those who proclaim the gospel must understand what such proclamation means and what acceptance of Christ means **in each piece of the vast human mosaic.** Read on.

Leaders of men constantly seek new patterns of life, win followers, and start new movements.

2

The Satnamis and
Unreached Peoples² Understood

This chapter deals with the Satnamis and their discipling. They were the unreached people. Any attempt to preach the gospel to them, and to encourage them to become followers of the Lord Jesus Christ and responsible members of His Church, must take the facts of this chapter into account.

The evangelisation and discipling of any unreached people in India or elsewhere must in similar fashion speak to a particular segment of society. Each segment has its own place of residence. It lives in this valley, that part of the province, the villages this side of the river or a certain section of the urban complex. It is known by a distinctive name. It has its own leaders, its own men of note, its own religious authorities and in some cases its own aristocracy. It usually has a distinct self-image. In sociological parlance, it is known as a clan, a caste, a tribe, a people, a minority, a distinct segment of mankind. While individual men and women will make the decision to become Christian, unless they win many others of their own segment to Christian faith, they are not likely to start a people movement. Only as they win multitudes of their own kind of people will unreached segments of society be discipled. This is true for all

---

² In this book "peoples" means castes, tribes, clans, segments of society. The Greek word for "peoples" is *ethne*. The Hindi word for "peoples" is *jatiyan*. "Peoples" in this book does **not** mean "individuals."

castes in India, high and low. It is true for every segment of
society in every country of the world.

Each segment has its subdivisions. Take the 2-million-
member Greek community in the United States. There are
fourth-generation men and women who know not a word of
Greek. There are Greeks descended from wealthy families and
those from poor peasant stock, those from the mountains of
northern Greece and those from the great metropolis of Athens.
There are Greeks who formed part of the Communist Party in
Greece during World War II and those who regarded the
Communists as traitors. Mankind exists not as a single
homogeneous whole but as a mosaic of thousands of pieces.

The Satnamis were one section of the Chamar community
and that, in turn, one section of the 80 million Untouchables
(1941 figures), now known as the Scheduled Castes and that in
turn one section of the Hindu community, which in 1988
numbered 700 million souls.

It is essential in any intelligent effort to enroll the peoples of
earth (in biblical terms, the *ethne*) under Christ's banner, to
recognise this mosaic and to evangelise and win to Christ each
of its pieces. If our kind of men and women are becoming
Christians and forming congregations, then we join that
movement far more readily than if we are invited to join a
conglomerate congregation in which there are many different
kinds of men and women.

**Thus, this story of the Satnamis ought to be read as an
illustration of evangelising each of the multitudinous pieces
of the mosaic.** Every unreached people must be recognised as a
separate unit. Its nature, history, composition, beliefs, likes and
dislikes all are part of the background, the context, to which the
Christian adjusts his message. The gospel must make sense to
one particular people, holding particular views, entertaining
particular prejudices and treasuring particular longings.

Americans have long entertained the idea that the many
different streams of immigrants would all in time (and the
sooner the better) become one new people—Americans. So
Americans find it difficult to recognise the particularity of each
of the multitudinous pieces of the mosaic. In Christ, American
Christians protest, are neither Jew nor Greek, slave nor free. The
glory of the Christian Church is that it is made up of individuals

of many ethnic units, all by the hot fire of the Holy Spirit being melted into one new people of God. Frank recognition of the mosaic and dedication to the evangelisation of each of its pieces seems to American Christians to be a distortion of the gospel. Any formation of clusters of congregations (conferences, unions, presbyteries) made up very largely of one kind of people, seems an unchristian process. "We are engaged," American Christians cry, "in a worldwide battle for brotherhood. We will not encourage recognition of different kinds of men and women. We will fight segregation in any form. We want conglomerate congregations and denominations, in which all are **one people**."

What shall we say to this serious objection? This is a most serious objection raised by Westerners and—unfortunately—by Western-educated Indian Christians. It is not, however, an objection which occurs to the multitudes of Christians in India who have come to Christ through a castewise movement to Christian faith. These recognise that while the ultimate goal is 100% brotherhood, **men and women like to be with their own kind of people.**

Recognising fully that all Christians are equally sons of Adam and sinners saved by grace, and fully committed to the extension of brotherhood, the church growth movement maintains that the best way to achieve brotherhood is to bring segment after segment of humanity into clusters of congregations of like-minded people—who speak the same language, eat the same kind of food at church suppers, dress the same way, hold similar longings and aspirations and feel comfortable in each other's presence. **This is the most effective way to achieve brotherhood.** Once the segment is thoroughly Christian, its prideful and sinful antagonisms toward other people groups will diminish. Once Christ is worshipped and obeyed, brotherhood increases. If on the other hand, instant brotherhood is demanded **before** Christ is received, when men lack the power to be brotherly, then brotherhood will not be achieved. Unsaved men and women do not believe in brotherhood.

Satnamis and the Caste System

Now, who are the Satnamis? In 1800, nearly 200 years ago, there were no Satnamis. About 1820 some Chamars became

Satnamis, and during the next hundred years several hundred thousand Chamars followed the Satnami faith. But who were the Chamars? They were one of numerous Untouchable castes. They had to live outside the Hindu village. They were not Hindus. Their caste duty was tanning hides—a dirty, odoriferous occupation. Many were landless labourers.

Historians agree that about 2000 B.C. the Aryans stormed in and gradually conquered India. Those dark-skinned Dravidians who submitted to them and accepted the status of inferiors (Shudra in Sanscrit means inferior) were accorded the rank of respectable serfs. Those who did not submit were ultimately conquered and made to do the most demeaning work—cleaning latrines, dragging the dead cattle out of the village, skinning them, making leather and other similar "untouchable" tasks.

The Untouchables occupied a position for many centuries outside Hinduism. They were not Brahmins. They were not Kshatriyas. They were not Vaishyas. They were not Shudras. They were down beneath all these castes as really non-Hindus. Their cluster of huts had to be built 100 yards away from the village. Until about 1920, Hindus went out of their way to say, "These people are not Hindus."

Then as self-governing India became a clear goal of all Indians, it became evident that if the Untouchables remained outside Hinduism, they would become Muslims or Christians. Some 60 or 80 million votes would go into the Christian or Muslim camp, and the Hindu voting block would be tremendously weakened. Thereupon Mahatma Gandhi and the people that he led, the Swaraj Party, began saying to the Untouchables, "You are Hindus. We love you. We're not going to allow you to become Christians." The Untouchables were by political leaders taken into the Hindu religion. They were counted as low Shudras. This only slightly elevated their position in society. The hide-gatherers, bone-gatherers, and latrine cleaners were still very humble people.

However, Gandhi, a political genius, on visiting a city, used to stay at one of their homes. Anyone who came to see him would have to come into the Untouchable quarters. The category "untouchable" was abolished. After 1940 they were called Harijans (God's people) and later—Scheduled Castes. Every strategy was used to say to these people, "You are part of the Hindu community."

The subcontinent of India with its 26,000 castes[3] is a wonderful example of the mosaic of mankind. The multitudinous pieces of this mosaic must be won to Christian faith if the Great Commission is to be carried out. The Great Commission clearly states that "all the *ethne*" are to be discipled. The *ethne* means the segments of humanity. The Greek word *ethnos* has always been translated in all Indian languages as *jati*.

The segmental nature of mankind is much larger than the caste system in India. A theory of world evangelisation that recognises *panta ta ethne*, all the segments of mankind, forms the last chapter in this book. After the account of the Satnami evangelisation has been completed, readers would do well to study the last chapter carefully and then reread the Satnami story. This story is not just an interesting account of missionary labours pertinent in all the world. The story is an attempted effective evangelism of a piece of the mosaic.

Pieces of the mosaic in South America, China or West Africa will certainly be different in many respects from the piece of the mosaic, the Satnamis, described in this book. Nevertheless, with minor changes the theory of effective evangelisation detailed in the last chapter in this book will be found applicable in all continents of the world, including Europe and North America.

Origin of the Chattisgarh Chamars

About 200 years before 1800 a band of Chamars grew very weary with the oppression under which they lived in the Gangetic Valley, the heart of Hinduism. Appalled at the Untouchable status that they "enjoyed," they decided to migrate 400 miles south to an area in the heart of India. It was surrounded by heavy jungles in which tigers and elephants

---

[3] David Barrett, ed., *World Christian Encyclopedia*. London: Oxford University Press, 1982, p. 371. If every group that marries strictly within itself is counted a caste, then David Barrett is unquestionably correct. If, however, the major castes are counted, each with many subcastes, of course, then 3,000 is a more reasonable figure.

roamed. Abundance of flat, fertile land was lying unused by anybody, covered by scrub jungle. The region was called Chattisgarh[4]. *Chhattis* means "36" and *garh* means "fort." This was the land of the 36 forts, which is simply a way of saying that it was a land of many small kingdoms. Any strong man who built a wall around his village became a king. There were Gond kings and Rawat kings and kings of other castes. There was continuous warfare to and fro. Land was laid waste. Tigers lived and hunted in river ravines and other patches of brambly jungle in the heart of the plain. *Sambar* (elk), *chital* (spotted deer), black buck, *nil gai* (giant antelope), and wild pigs were very common. Nobody got a crop unless he guarded it night and day from the time the grain sprouted until the time it was harvested.

Into this land came the Chamars. The plain itself was quite extensive—200 miles long and 150 miles wide. It was well watered by about 40 inches of rainfall mostly in the months of July, August and September.

The black cotton clay was exceedingly fertile. If it was ploughed and cultivated and guarded from the wild animals, it gave good crops. True, there were dangers. In addition to the animals mentioned there were wolves, wild dogs (red dogs, they were called), panthers, bears, and python. About 1840 the last elephant herd was driven into a *kheddah* and tamed.

Free land was the chief attraction. The feudal lord welcomed anybody who would settle on his land, cutting down the scrub jungle, braving sickness and wild animals, and enduring the occasional year of drought when peasants would harvest little and die in great numbers.

In some cases the Chamars took up land in existing villages where the malguzar or feudal lord said, "Yes, you are welcome. Cultivate that land." In some cases, a band of Chamars got a new section of land and their headman was recognised as a new feudal lord himself. So in Chattisgarh there came to be Untouchable feudal lords—a very strange thing in Hindu India. These malguzars owned hundreds of acres. Their more industrious peasants each owned ten or twenty acres of land. The less industrious or fortunate owned only two or three acres, or none at all.

---

[4] See dotted-line section on map facing p. 1.

This was a big change from the landless leather tanners and the Achchhut (Untouchables) of the Gangetic valley, whose duty was to drag the dead cattle out of the village, a task no Vaishya, Shudra, Kshatriya, or Brahmin cultivator would dream of doing. He called a Chamar to drag out his dead ox or cow. Dead and stinking animals belonged to the Chamar, who took off the hide and cut off such meat as he wished to eat. He cooked and ate some. He dried some. The rest was eagerly devoured by the dogs and vultures by day and hyenas and jackals by night. The Chamar was regarded as a very low piece of humanity, really not quite human—certainly not a Hindu.

When the Chamars entered Chattisgarh, they got free land. Dragging the dead cattle out of the village and tanning hides was not their main task. They made a tremendous leap upward in the economic scale. However, they still felt that cow meat was a rather nice thing to eat. It gave strength. It was cheap. And in times of famine, when the grain harvest failed and the cattle died for lack of pasture, it was fortunate to be able to prolong life with cow meat, even though that made you an Untouchable.

In 1800, in Chattisgarh there were maybe 50,000, maybe 200,000 Chamars. A few of them were feudal lords. The caste had developed an aristocracy whose members composed the "first families." Often these were owners of whole villages. When a Chamar aristocrat married his sons and daughters, he tended to marry them to the offspring of other leading families. So, a kind of an aristocracy grew up amongst them. Yet they remained Chamars, and they ate cow meat. Of course, they were still scorned by all Hindus, whether these were Vaishyas, Brahmins, Kshatriyas or Shudras.

The first Chamar settlements took place along the rivers, where there was good water twelve months of the year. The women would go down to the river and bring big pots of water back on their heads, sufficient for cooking and washing. A daily bath in the river was a way of keeping clean. However, because the river sites were always at a premium and the Chamars were recent immigrants, to get free land they often had to press on to interior sites far away from any river, where the plain had no stream flowing through it. In each such interior site the Chamars built a *talao* or man-made lake two to twenty acres in size. They put a big dike across some low place, dug out the land back of it to get the earth for the dike, and thus made a *talao*. Into it, during the rains, flowed the rainfall from a large acreage. In this fashion, year-round water became available and the whole plain gradually became populated. Between A.D. 1600 and 1800 other castes—Gonds, Rawats, Agharias, and others—were also migrating into Chattisgarh.

Satnami Beginnings

About 1817, a Chamar peasant named Ghasi Das lived near the centre of the great plain some distance south and east of Raipur in a village called Bhandar. He went on a pilgrimage to the river Ganges, probably to where Calcutta stands today. It was 400 miles to the east. The fact that he made such a pilgrimage on foot indicates that he was a man of religious sensitivity. There on the banks of one of the mouths of the Ganges, called the Hoogli, he heard William Carey or some other missionary. He came back with a striking message for the Chamars. It was a call to become a new people. Because of their unusual landed nature, his message found immediate and widespread acceptance. He cried, "Throw out your idols. Worship only the true God. Quit eating meat—neither cow meat nor pig meat nor deer meat nor goat meat nor chicken meat. **Eat no meat.** It lowers you in the estimate of the Hindus. Quit keeping chickens, or you'll be tempted to eat them, and thus lower the status of our whole caste. Dress in white. Live simply. You're not to eat out of brass vessels or wear brightly coloured clothing. Wait for the coming of a red-faced man with a big hat on his head and a big book in his hand. Do what he tells you."

When the Chamars asked, "What is the name of the true God whom you proclaim?" Ghasi Das replied, "I do not know, but it is the True Name."

In Hindi, "true" is *sat* and "name" is *nam*. So "true name" became *sat nam*. They became the worshippers of Satnam, the True Name. They called themselves True Namers, or Satnamis. When they met somebody, they did not say "Good morning" or "Good evening"—"Salam" or "Bandagi." They said "Satnam." Thus was the Satnami caste born.

It was a religious revival of considerable size. Not only did the Chamars follow Ghasi Das in great numbers, but also a few hundred Telis did. Their caste duty is extracting oil from seed.

Telis were respectable Shudras. Some hundreds of them became followers of the True Name. They did not intermarry with the Chamars, but did throw out their idols and become True Namers.

While the Satnami religion and the new Satnam caste spread like wildfire amongst the Chamars, it did not win all of them. Certain sections of the Chamar population formed distinct subcastes of their own. In 1917, about 100 years after all this began, there was a caste of about 50,000 called Chungia Chamars. *Chungi* is a pipe. Members of this Chamar subcaste smoked tobacco. Ghasi Das had told his followers not to smoke tobacco and not to drink liquor. However, the Chungia Chamars saw nothing wrong with tobacco. They liked to smoke it. They continued the old ways. Some of them gave up eating meat, and some of them did not, but all of them smoked.

Then there were the Kanaujia Chamars. These continued the practice of tanning hides. They could make a good living out of it. They also gathered up bones and sold them. They dried the meat of the dead animals they skinned. They were convinced meat eaters. Kanaujias in general had a good physique. Adding meat to one's diet does increase physical strength.

Some of the Satnamis were called Jahari. These were the zealots, the hundred-percenters. These wore only white clothing. They ate only out of earthenware vessels. They did not have brass plates or brass pots. They had no idols whatever in their homes.

Continuing Hindu Influence

Despite the widespread acceptance of the Satnami religion, the fact that Satnamis had no sacred book and in the beginning were almost entirely illiterate left them with a great vacuum. By 1920 as some of their more intelligent young men learned how to read—usually in mission schools—a strange thing happened. These literate young men, as a means of earning good money, started copying the Hindu pundits. The story is well worth recounting.

Hindu pundits (learned priests) would frequently buy a Bhagavad-Gita. This was a ponderous tome five inches thick, fifteen inches long and ten inches wide. They would then persuade some wealthy Hindu in a village to pay them several hundred rupees for reading the Bhagavad-Gita aloud night after night for a week or ten days in or near his house. The Brahmin pundit would build an earthen platform in a place where the crowd could assemble. There night after night seated on the platform with the impressive tome before him he would read aloud the Bhagavad-Gita. He was well paid for this. The man who paid him to read was assured that he would get very substantial reward in good crops or more children. The Satnamis, however, because they were Untouchables were not allowed to attend these readings. All they could do was to sit in the far fringes of the crowd separate from the Hindus by at least ten feet.

The literate Satnami young men—the ablest of them—said to themselves, "We will buy a Bhagavad-Gita. We will build a platform in the Satnami section (generally just outside the village). We will get some of the well-to-do Satnamis to pay us a fee of several hundred rupees, and night after night for eight or ten nights we will read aloud an impressive book, just like the Hindus."

Thus the Satnamis were gradually pulled back into idolatry. Most of them had really never left it. When smallpox raged, they offered milk to the idol of the smallpox goddess. They also sacrificed to the deity of the fields before sowing them.

In a similar fashion the Ramayan was read by Brahmins for the Hindus, so the literate Satnamis began earning good money by reading it aloud to Satnami audiences in the Satnami sections of the village. This was not considered idolatry. It was thought to be high religion. Since, however, both books are full of the names of many gods, it was in fact active idolatry.

The Satnamis also copied another Hindu worship form. This was called Rahas Lila. In March at the beginning of the long dry season, a Hindu pundit—for a fat fee—would make ten or twenty idols of mud, some of them more than life-size. As soon as they were dry, he would paint them with gaudy colors. Here eight feet tall stood the great incarnation, Ram. Here was the monkey god, Hanuman, with his long tail. Here was the goddess Sita, and up and down the village lane many, many others.

Then, when everything was ready and the whole village had with great interest watched these idols being made, the Rahas Lila (the Sport of Pleasure) would begin. The pundit would recite stories from behind his altar or podium. The village crowd, coming and going, would look and listen. A few of the more knowledgeable men would join in the better known choruses. The Rahas lasted a week or more. In some of the night sessions after the love affairs of the gods were recited, the young men and women would slip out of the village to indulge in sexual intercourse.

When the rainy season came, these gods and goddesses gradually disintegrated—and were a drab and sorry sight for many months. Ghasi Das had ridiculed these gods; however, in the 20th century, the Satnamis began to make these mud gods in many of their stronger villages. The peasant who called a Satnami pundit and paid him several hundred rupees, was, they believed, sure to gain much merit and to obtain what he wished.

It was amongst these Satnamis—a monotheistic sect that had gradually become polytheistic—that Christ was proclaimed. Ghasi Das" message inclined them to the Christian faith. However, their Hindu surroundings militated against it. That was the background. We must therefore ask, Did Satnamis in this particular state of religious belief become Christian?

When Ghasi Das returned to Chattisgarh about 1817, he found no missionaries. The missionaries were still a long way off—400 miles to the east in Bengal or 300 miles to the southeast in Orissa. They did not penetrate to Chattisgarh for many years.

Furthermore, when Ghasi Das died about 1840, one of his sons became the guru and inherited the adulation and reverence tendered to his father. It was said that when Ghasi Das went out to cultivate his fields carrying his plough on his shoulder—as all peasants do—and driving his oxen before him, his plough did not rest on his shoulder. He felt no weight. It floated in the air six inches above his shoulder. As he progressed, his plough floated along with him. Many other stories of the magical power of Ghasi Das circulated amongst the Satnamis and no doubt grew in the telling.

Then the second guru's son and after him his son became gurus. These men found themselves in positions of very great power. Perhaps 100,000 people regarded the guru as their spiritual leader. It was a very fortunate occurrence if the guru visited a Satnami's home. As the guru toured around to hundreds of villages in Chattisgarh, he collected a rupee from each family.

The guru was particularly welcome in the villages where there were Satnami feudal lords (malguzars); there he was treated like a king. Thus the guru received an assured income of perhaps 100,000 rupees a year. Many gifts were made. Ghasi Das' sons became men of considerable wealth. One of them, a man of genius, thought, "Let me buy an elephant. Kings ride on elephants. I can buy an elephant and ride up to my people **on an elephant.** This high status conforms well with my exalted position."

So he bought an elephant and hired an elephant keeper. In 1850 it cost nothing to feed an elephant, which tore branches off trees and ate them. Often also the *mahout* would cut branches off the trees and feed them to his huge animal. In addition, the guru's elephant received offerings of chapatis—unleavened, whole wheat bread—and other gifts in the villages.

The gurus became men of very great power. As they travelled from village to village, they got food and lodging and any women they might choose to spend the night with. All this happened before the missionaries arrived.

The First Missionaries Come to Chattisgarh

Between 1820 and 1860 the English government was extending its rule into the heart of India which it called Central Provinces. It divided up Central Provinces into divisions and put an Englishman of great ability in charge of each. The administrator sent to Chattisgarh in the southeast corner of Central Provinces lived at Raipur. See map on the following page. He began sending back word through official and unofficial channels that a great number in Chattisgarh were looking forward to the coming of the white man.

A district commissioner as he toured the villages was frequently asked, "Are you the white man with the big book in his hand who is supposed to come?"

"No," he'd say, "I'm not he. I have no big book in my hand. I am a government official."

Some of these officials were earnest Christians. They sent word to the Anglicans and the Presbyterians, saying, "Here is a district into which some missionary ought to come soon."

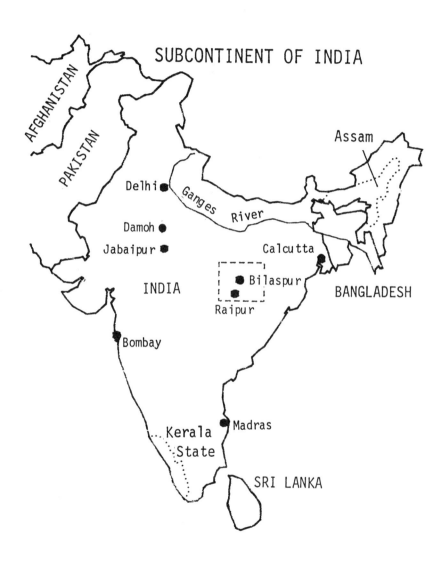

SUBCONTINENT OF INDIA

AFGHANISTAN

PAKISTAN

Assam

Delhi

Ganges River

Damoh

Jabaipur

Calcutta

INDIA

Bilaspur

BANGLADESH

Raipur

Bombay

Kerala State

Madras

SRI LANKA

The first mission board to respond was that founded by the Foreign Mission Board of the Evangelical Synod of North America with headquarters in St Louis, in the United States. Its members were of German descent. In 1860-65 they sent pioneer missionaries to Raipur, the divisional headquarters of Chattisgarh. These missionaries immediately contacted the Satnamis, but when the ruling guru found that being Christian meant living a holy life and that the missionaries had no intention of allowing the profligate guru the exalted position he had, he and his *mahants* (bishops) turned solidly against Christianity.

One wonders what would have happened if the missionaries, believing that as Christianity spread morals would improve, had simply said, "You all become Christians. Your guru and his executives will become archbishop and bishops. The archbishop and bishops will continue to have their present prerogatives and powers."

In this day of contextualization a thought like that is attractive. However, had this been put to those early missionaries, they would have said, "These men are monotheists, at least in part, but they are also avaricious, rapacious, sinful men. They are adulterers on a very large scale. They manifest a high degree of corruption, deceit and worship of wealth and of sex. All this is a denial of Christ. Any turning to Christ must be an honest, sincere and biblical turning. Consequently, as we present Christianity to them, we must insist that they leave their sinful way of life and follow the straight and narrow path."

As a result, there was no massive turning of the Satnamis to Christian faith. While for the next 100 years the gospel was listened to with great interest and much verbal agreement by the Satnamis, the number who became Christians was always small.

The evangelical missionaries began their first work in the city of Raipur. Traveling by oxcart and foot they visited the guru's village, Bhandar, the Mecca of the Satnamis. They proclaimed Christ in hundreds of villages as they toured. Everywhere they were heard with keen interest. A Satnami people movement to Christ seemed imminent. However, such was the power of the gurus and so strong was the caste system that a large people movement never took place. Any families who became Christians were promptly outcasted. No one would eat with them, receive a cup of water from them, give them a daughter in marriage, or work as a labourer for them. To become a Christian was—the guru's family held—to become another caste, totally separate from the Satnamis.

As stated, the missionaries first lived in the city of Raipur. Some years later, as famines and crop failures occurred they bought 1200 acres 50 miles east of Raipur at a place they called Bishrampur, the City of Rest. As they toured the district and proclaimed Christ in many villages, small groups of Satnamis decided to follow Christ. Since the Satnami power structure outcasted them, the converts moved to Bishrampur. There the feudal lord, the mission, gave them land, and they continued their life of cultivation.

This moving to the mission station became the pattern because the gurus had vigorously turned against the Christian faith. Any Satnami or group of Satnamis becoming Christian was promptly ostracised. If any Satnami ate with a Christian, drank with him, gave him a daughter in marriage, or took a daughter-in-law from him, he was ostracised. The small groups of Satnami converts were effectively boycotted. Since the power of the feudal lords was very great and the ostracism was complete, Christians found it difficult to continue living in their village. If an ox of a Christian cultivator died, no one loaned him an ox and his field was uncultivated. If a convert died, no one buried his body. If a single family only had become Christian in a distant village, the body lay there and stunk for some days until his widow could send to Bishrampur. Then a party of Christians came out, dug a grave, and buried the body. The whole caste machinery was arrayed against leaving the Satnami caste and joining the Christian caste!

This defence mechanism is used against Christianity by every caste in India—and to a lesser degree by most segments of society in all six continents. Discipling *panta ta ethne* means finding ways through the defence. **If an ethnic unit is to be won, ways must be found for men and women to become Christian while remaining loyal affectionate members of their segments of society.**

Despite these obstacles, across the next hundred years in the evangelical missions and four other missions which began work in Chattisgarh some thousands did become Christians.

For many years there was a tug of war between two groups of missionaries. One felt that enough Satnamis would eventually become Christian so that there would be a substantial movement to Christ from within the Satnami caste. The second group, through direct evangelism, mission schools, mission hospitals, and other forms of indirect evangelism, worked for Respectable Caste men and women to become Christian.

The first hoped that these Satnami Christians would continue to live in the villages as still ethnically Satnamis and that their worship and their Book would commend Christ to the Satnamis. Gradually more and more Satnamis would become Christian. A castewise movement to Christ would occur. This, however, never happened. The whips of ostracism were too cutting. Christians to live at all had to flee to the city of refuge. A strong Christian community grew up at Bishrampur. Similar communities grew up at all mission stations, but all who lived there were regarded by the Satnamis (and all Hindus) as a new caste, Christians.

Missionaries From the Christian Churches Arrive

In 1882, a party of missionaries of the denomination in America known as Christian Churches/Disciples of Christ arrived in India. The family and two single ladies settled in Harda, about 400 miles east of Bombay, on the railway being driven through from Bombay to Allahabad and then on down to Calcutta. In Harda they heard about the Satnamis who were "waiting for the coming of a red-faced man with a big book in his hand."

In 1884, the next party of their missionaries proceeded on the railway to Jabalpur. There they bought oxcarts and walked 200 miles in a slightly south-easterly direction through the forests of the Mandla District, a very rough and wild territory. They were headed to the great plain of Chattisgarh.

On a couple of occasions, tigers crossed the road in front of the little caravan of seven carts and disappeared into the jungle. The men and the women usually walked. Their goods were carried on the carts. A wheel would break, and the whole party would wait until it was repaired. When it rained, they would pitch the tent and wait until the downpour had ended. The men had guns. They shot deer and supplemented the boiled rice and chapatis with deer meat.

Finally they came out into the plains of Chattisgarh, some 70 miles west of Bilaspur, the headquarters town of the Bilaspur District. It lay 25 miles east of Bishrampur. The road leading to it was simply a track, which after every rain was very muddy. The oxen were accustomed to this, and making two miles an hour or less they would patiently pull the carts along.

Finally the party reached Bilaspur. There the missionaries bought land and started building places to live. It was impossible to rent. The only way was to buy a piece of land, not usually easy, and then build on it. They couldn't buy land in the town itself; nobody would sell land to Christians. So they bought it outside of town, a half a mile away, and there erected their first bungalows. The ladies' bungalow was built about a half a mile from the bungalow of the family. The work started.

The Satnamis gave them very much the same response they had given to the missionaries of the Evangelical Synod. Because they were red-faced men with a big book, they were listened to with interest. However, because Christianity was a different religion, had its own standards, would not allow the gurus with their profligate ways of life to be the religious leaders of the church, Christianity was rejected even though it had received considerable acclaim from the Satnamis. They liked the fact that Christians had no idols and that Christianity maintained there was no caste, that all men were children of Adam and hence brothers. However, the moral demands and the fact that Christianity had no place in it for a hereditary guruship made it almost impossible for the Satnami *ethnos* (*jati*) to consider becoming Christian.

The missionary must understand the tribe, caste, or class to which God has sent him.

3

One Unreached People, the Satnamis, Evangelised

The Bilaspur District to which the Christian Church missionaries came lay north and east of the Bishrampur/Raipur District occupied by the Evangelical and Reformed Mission. As each new mission came into India, it went to an unoccupied part of that great subcontinent.

The town of Bilaspur (district headquarters) lay 25 miles northeast of Bishrampur. From Bilaspur the main road of the district ran straight west 30 miles to Mungeli, the headquarters of the Mungeli subdistrict.

The First Explorers

The first missionary in the Mungeli area was George Jackson, a Wesleyan from England, who came to believe that baptism should be by immersion, and so joined the missionaries of the Christian Churches of America living at Bilaspur. He lived there 1884-86 while acquiring land and building a bungalow at Mungeli, where he lived for the next four years. He toured the district continuously. His diary tells of going 70 miles north through great jungles to Pendra, and then on another 30 miles to the pilgrimage center of Amarkantak. Another time he loaded up his oxcart and walked 80 miles east to Korba. Still another tour was west to Lormi. His journal contains entries such as the following:

> Ganiari was a waste of time. No one listened. . . In Amarkantak the pilgrims listened with rapt attention. I must try to get back here, though the road is difficult. . . . . A sick Brahmin in Mungeli read the

Gospel of John through in one day. He seems very
open to the gospel. I must return here some day.

George Jackson, who spent at least ten hours a day when not
on tour in the study of Hindi, had a severe break of health in
1890 and left the field, never to return. But he had convinced his
missionary colleagues that the field was well worth developing.
He had built a comfortable bungalow at Mungeli, won a few
converts and left three employees to look after the mission
property. In 1892, the mission sent young John Grafton
McGavran there. He had arrived in India in October 1891, four
months after graduating from college. He was temporarily
located at Harda. In February of 1892 he was sent to Mungeli.
He continued the exploration.

Mungeli was a small town of about 4,000 inhabitants. It was
the headquarters of the *tahasil* or subdistrict of Bilaspur, and had
a police station, a post office and a minor court. It was 30 miles
off the railway to the west of Bilaspur, the district headquarters.
In those days there was no motor transport. To get from
Bilaspur to Mungeli took two days by oxcart or horse *tonga*.

When in 1892 John McGavran arrived in Bilaspur, an
unmarried man of 26, he knew his work was the evangelisation
of the villages. The plain immediately surrounding Bilaspur was
being evangelised by the missionary at Bilaspur. However,
immediately around Mungeli and away to the north and west and
20 miles to the south was a vast untouched population. Villages
occurred every half mile or so, and while wild animals were
plentiful, the plain was full of people. British India extended
some 20 miles west of Mungeli. Next to it was the native state of
Kawardha. This was open to evangelisation. The raja was
friendly to missionaries. He probably considered the missionary
enterprise a part of British rule.

Hira Lal, a highly intelligent young Satnami who had become
a Christian before 1890 all by himself, had never been to school
but knew how to read and write. He formed part of the group of
Indian helpers who toured with John McGavran. Touring meant
loading tents and other equipment onto a cart at the beginning of
the day and taking them off at about four o'clock in the
afternoon at another village. There the tents would be pitched
under a tree. Camp would be set up and a meal cooked. For

several days the missionary and his helpers walked to and preached in nearby villages.

Exploration of a new field was, is and will be the beginning stage of all attempts to evangelise unreached peoples. Touring, such as that done by George Jackson and John McGavran, was common practice among the missionaries of all denominations all over India. The land and its peoples had to be explored. No one knew who—if any—would on hearing the gospel become Christians. The task was to preach widely, sow the seed everywhere and trust that those chosen by God would respond. Sometimes this might be a Brahmin or one of the ruling caste or a devout cultivator or some wandering seeker—a *sadhu.*

Let me illustrate this by the story of a convert won in the far west of India, 500 miles from Chattisgarh. In the 1870's there lived a young Brahmin into whose hands came a copy of the New Testament. He read it and was captivated by the Lord Jesus. He thought of himself as a *chela* (disciple) of Jesus, the Guru. He walked 25 miles to the district headquarters, sought out the Presbyterian missionary and was baptised. In 1923, he, an old man then, was my Hindi teacher, as I studied the Hindi language in the Landour language school in the Himalayas. He said to me one day: "If I had met Christians before reading the Bible, I would never have become a Christian. But thank God I read the Bible first. Only later did I learn that Christians ate meat and even ate beef!" He was, of course, outcasted by his family.

Many other examples could be given of men of high and low estate who, one by one, for various reasons became Christians. Some were servants of a missionary and had daily instruction. Some were sick and were healed by the Christians, and so drew close and finally became Christians. Some, like my teacher, were intelligent, devout converts. Some were rebels in their families and open to "become something else." They listened to the gospel long enough to believe it. No one could know where such people might be found. So, widespread preaching and sowing the seed across a whole district was standard missionary practice.

In addition, practical considerations ruled. Missionaries (whether nationals of that land or foreigners from abroad) ought to live at some centre of population where they could reach many, and from which they could come and go. They should settle in towns to which mail was delivered and where suitable land for building could be purchased.

Today the last two decades of the 20th century and on into the 21st, reaching unreached peoples for Christ will inevitably involve a great deal of exploratory work. Not only must each unreached people—whether urban or rural—be recognised as a distinct unit of society, but it must be explored, learned, tested and systematically evangelised. Its desire to hear the gospel must be measured. The likelihood that enough men and women of one *ethnos* will become openly baptised Christians must be estimated. Lists of names of those who welcome the missionary, who say, "Come back again and let us hear this good news," must be compiled. What **groups** seem to have been chosen by the Lord to lead the march out of the land of bondage must be ascertained.

The exploratory work in the Mungeli area, begun by George Jackson and continued by John McGavran, whose story forms the heart of this chapter, must be seen as typical of what is to be done in every unreached people. True, by a careful study of the history of missions in that general population, the years of exploration may be shortened; however, it would be unwise to count on great shortening. Times change, and we must determine what segments of the population God has **now** prepared, and what methods He is **now** blessing to the multiplication of churches. Effective evangelisation involves conscientious, intelligent exploration. Now back to the Satnami story.

Hira Lal was a highly intelligent man, spoke the language well, and knew the people. He was not above carrying the load of books or other materials, such as boiled water to drink throughout the day and a "magic lantern" to show pictures at night.

The Satnamis were friendly, but John McGavran preached more to the upper and middle castes. In those early days, missionaries did not know the caste system well, and to John McGavran all villagers were people who needed Christ. He held the common opinion that the best way to reach the whole population was by winning the leaders; so, while he did on occasion preach in Satnami villages and while the Satnamis came to his meetings in the respectable sections of other villages, sitting on the far edges of the crowd, he did not concentrate on them. However, Hira Lal, a Satnami by caste, did speak to them. They heard him with considerable interest. The message of Ghasi Das was fresh in their minds. They believed that any knowledge about Satnam, the True Name, the only God, was worth listening to.

Interesting Incidents of Exploration

In those days there were plenty of wild animals. Deer were plentiful. Sections of jungle were common all across the plain. To the north a range of jungle-covered hills rose a couple of thousand feet above the plain. Sometimes the jungle areas lay along rivers or between villages. All of these were the havens of wild animals. Herds of antelope, wild pig, and packs of wolves were often seen. Lone panthers, tigers and hyenas prowled at night. On one occasion, when John McGavran's tent had been pitched on one side of a *talao*, or artificial pond, a pack of wild dogs chasing a *sambar* (elk) pulled it down on the far bank of the *talao*. While they tore the body and ate it greedily, pushing one another and trying to get through to the carcass, suddenly a tiger appeared on the scene. The red dogs, with one accord, without argument, left. The tiger came up to the carcass and began to eat.

On another occasion John McGavran shot three ducks sitting on a *talao*. There they lay, 20 yards from the bank. He turned to the villagers, who had come to see what was happening, and said, "Someone swim out there and bring me the ducks. I'll pay you."

They replied, "No! There's a god, a *dev*, who pulls under anyone who swims there. Nobody swims in that *talao*."

John McGavran asked them, "You mean there's a big alligator in there, a man eater?"

"Oh no," they replied. "There is no alligator in this pond, but there is a god and he does pull people under."

At this, John McGavran thought, "If I swim out there and get these ducks and come back unscathed, this will destroy their belief in that god. Just to make sure, I'll take the extra precaution of putting a board under my chest. Buoyed up in part on that, I'll swim out, get the ducks and come back." So, telling them that there was no god there, that their fears were groundless, and that he would demonstrate it, he launched out into the *talao.*

He had not gone 15 feet before he felt slimy weed clinging around his feet and legs. The *talao* was full of weeds that grew to within a foot of the surface. The only way to go out and get those ducks and come back without being dragged under by the weeds—that is, by the *dev*—was to swim on the surface and not let his legs get entangled. He swam on the surface, got the ducks, and came back to the shore.

The outcome was not what he expected. Instead of joyfully declaring, "There is no god there," they immediately said, "This man is a god himself. He's a bigger god than the other. He has more power." Then they brought a chicken from the village and sacrificed it to him.

This event indicates the adventure a missionary may run into, and also the tremendous animistic substratum of belief that underlay and still underlies both Satnamism and Hinduism.

Any missionary who tours the villages continually risks infection. Even though missionaries in those days boiled their drinking water and slept under nets, there was considerable danger that one way or another they would get infected. Missionaries did not put a net on when addressing a village crowd after dark. When they sat quietly as somebody else read the Scriptures or when they were talking to visitors, the mosquitoes feasted on their ankles.

In 1893, John McGavran came down with a high, prolonged fever. Whether it was typhoid or malaria or some other disease, he never knew. He barely made it back to Mungeli. There, for some weeks, his life hung by a thread. Finally, the high fever departed. The mission sent him up to the hill station of Darjeeling to recuperate. Darjeeling lay at 7,000 feet and had a cool, comfortable climate. He got on the train at Bilaspur and went east 400 miles to Calcutta, and from there, north 300 miles by train to the foothills beneath Darjeeling, and then by horse up the mountain. There he met a Baptist missionary, James Henry Anderson, whose 22-year-old daughter had come out from England to visit her parents. John McGavran and Helen Anderson became acquainted. She then went back to England. Correspondence between John and Helen resulted in their engagement. In September 1895 she travelled by steamer to Bombay, where she and John McGavran were married.

Exploration Ceases

In 1894, the mission, facing a widespread famine, decided to open a central boys orphanage. It said,

> We can't start orphanages in every station. This mission's boys orphanage will be in Damoh, some 300 miles north of Mungeli. We're going to send all orphan boys from all stations to Damoh. We want you, John McGavran, to go to Damoh. It's a new station and has great opportunities. You must leave your work at Mungeli and Kawardha and go to Damoh.

Majority rule was and is regular policy in most missions. The location of a missionary does not depend exclusively upon his own wishes but upon the judgement of the mission. Since there were several senior missionaries who had gotten to India two, three or even ten years before John McGavran and since he had been in the country only three years, his wishes in the matter were overruled. He believed that God wanted him to work in the Chattisgarh plain, open the native state of Kawardha and establish a mission station there. But the mission said, "No, we can't spread out that far. We already have missionaries in Mungeli and Bilaspur. You must go to Damoh and help establish a new station there."

John went to Damoh. When in September 1895 he married Helen Anderson in Bombay—she had come out from England by sea—he took her straight to Damoh. The famine was raging. He had built a grass hut, about 10 by 15 feet in size, it floor about a foot off the ground; thus the floor would not get wet when it rained. There they lived, and there my sister Grace was born in November 1896. By the time I was born in December 1897, my father had rented and moved into a bungalow built by an Anglo-Indian—a big permanent structure.

I have spoken of John McGavran's contact with the Satnamis only to say that it was that kind of contact that several of the Christian Church missionaries had. They explored the field. They toured. They won a few individuals and a few small groups of Satnamis. Most of the individuals were forced out of the villages and came to live at or near the mission stations. A few small groups of converts, however, braving ostracism, stayed in their villages. The Satnamis as a whole were not responsive.

A Castewise Movement Almost Begins

The next notable incident in the evangelisation of the Satnamis came between 1914 and 1917. Partly as a side effect of World War I, the Satnami community was in great turmoil. In addition to the Satnami Chamars, the Chungia Chamars were numerous around Mungeli. Later they became Satnamis, but in 1914 they were still smoking tobacco and considered themselves a separate caste. They were down toward the bottom of the social scale and yet among them were powerful men who were malguzars of whole villages. A few others were owners of 20, 30, 40 acres. Many others owned small acreages. Many were landless.

These 50,000 Chamars had leaders in maybe 20 villages—men of note who formed a kind of aristocracy. Between 1914 and 1917, a movement developed amongst them. A common mind appeared which said, "Instead of becoming Satnamis, let us become Christians. That is a better way up."

They welcomed missionary Grainger. They began to say among themselves, "Why stay Chungia Chamars? Becoming Christian is a good step to take."

Some would argue on the other side, "No, indeed, it's not a good step." However, the mood grew increasingly favourable. The aristocrats more and more frequently said quietly to each other, "Let's think about it. Let's hear the gospel. Let's make some conditions. Let's tell the missionary that we're interested."

One of the chief factors in the creation of this mind was Hira Lal, the Satnami convert of 1888. By 1914 he had become an able man. The missionary doctor appointed him as assistant in the hospital. He watched the doctor doing operations, taking out cataracts and giving medicine. He soon came to know what medicines you gave for what sicknesses. He handed the doctor the various instruments used in taking cataracts out of eyes. Hira Lal said to himself, "I could do that." When the mission doctor went on furlough, he said to Hira Lal, "You're in charge of the hospital, and where you feel that you can give medicine safely, by all means give it. I'll be back in 18 months."

Hira Lal not only gave medicines; he also performed cataract and other minor operations. As a result, he came to be called Dr Hira Lal.

His house became a stopping place for the leaders of the Chungia Chamars when they came to town, sometimes to shop and sometimes to bear witness in a law case, or to sue or be sued. They were constantly walking five, ten, or twenty miles from their villages to Mungeli, the headquarters of the subdistrict. It had a court of law, a police station and other government offices. When their work at the governmental offices or the bazaar was finished, these leaders (particularly those who lived ten or more miles away) instead of walking home, would stop to chat with Hira Lal. He would say to them, "Why don't you spend the night here? Here's a room and a bed. Build a fire and cook your food. Then sleep here."

Dr Hira Lal was a friend. Listening to him read the Bible, they came to have a better understanding of the Christian faith. One of his great merits was that he knew the New Testament. He knew where to find passages. He would turn to a verse that fitted the occasion. The New Testament in his hands was a Living Book—the Book Ghasi Das had said the white man would bring. To be sure, they heard it in Hindi and their mother tongue was not Hindi, but Chattisgarhi. Still, they understood it.

Through missionary Grainger's and Dr Hira Lal's work the idea spread. Preaching in scores of villages and giving magic lantern lectures on the life of Christ reached thousands. In each village, hundreds would assemble and see the pictures and hear interesting expositions of the good news. The conviction spread among them, "Let's all become Christians. This is a very good thing to do." The movement climaxed in 1917.

The leaders of the Chungias called a great gathering at Set Ganga,[5] where a small brook welled up out of the plain and flowed away to the east. Since water does not ordinarily well up out of the earth, they believed that some spiritual force was at work. Set Ganga was a holy place.

---

[5] Set Ganga is a half mile north of Fosterpur. See Fosterpur on the map.

Hindus had built a small temple there hundreds of years before. As in many other Hindu temples they had placed twelve carved stones around the doorway and on its sides. These depicted naked men and women having sexual intercourse. Set Ganga was a famous place. It was there that the Chungia Chamars decided to hold a great conference in April 1917 after the crops had been harvested. There they assembled to consider becoming Christian as a whole people. The Christian evangelist, Dr Hira Lal, was there. The Chungias heard him with rapt attention. Then they said, "You can go now. We'll talk this over amongst ourselves. We have resolved to leave idolatry. Ghasi Das told us to do this a hundred years ago. Just when we leave, however, remains to be decided."

The Hindus, however, had also heard about this gathering of Chungias to decide to become Christian. How could the Hindus help but hear this talk among the Chamars, the lowest caste in the plain—in many cases their serfs? To the Hindus, the idea of the Chamars becoming Christians was utterly abhorrent. The Hindus felt they were losing their serfs to the Christians, the white men who were the rulers of the country. The self-government movement under Gandhi was beginning to get under way. It was not nearly so strong as it would be in a few years, but the Hindi newspapers were talking excitedly about *swaraj* (self-government) in the days when England was fighting for its life against Germany. There was considerable speculation amongst the intelligentsia as to India becoming totally free as soon as Britain was defeated. They did not realise that if Britain was defeated, the Germans would rule India.

Consequently, the Mungeli subinspector of police, a zealous Hindu (the highest police officer in that subdistrict), went to Set Ganga. He pitched his tent 200 yards from the Chungia Chamar encampment; he was not going to defile himself by living amongst them. He then summoned the leading men to come to him one by one. He said to each, "Remember, if you become Christian, I'm going to make sure that that case against you where I was lenient is taken up again. If you become Christian, then when other people charge you with offences, I shall do a very thorough investigation. I've been good to you people, but remember that I can be very harsh. Do you understand? If you become Christians, you will go to jail."

The Chungia Chamars were a timid people. While they had an aristocracy and while a few of them owned large amounts of land, they were, after all, Chamars, Untouchables. They were the victims of the Hindu social order. Consequently, as they considered becoming Christian, they did what such people normally do—deferred decision. They said, "We won't make a decision here at Set Ganga. We won't anger our subinspector of police. Next year we'll meet and decide then."

The moment had passed. The frame of mind that said, "Let's become Christian," was permanently stopped. A few years later they decided to become Satnamis, because the Satnamis were still in the Hindu fold. The few literate Satnamis read the Ramayan and the Bhagavad-Gita. Because of a rapidly fading monotheism, the Satnamis actually worshipped Hindu idols and went on pilgrimages to Hindu shrines. Their monotheism had been superficial. The possibility of a united Chungia movement to Christian faith grew less and less.

Other Small Beginnings

While this was happening amongst the Chungias at Mungeli and Fosterpur—30 and 40 miles west of Bilaspur—something else was happening in the Bilaspur field. There, some of the Satnamis were turning in small numbers to the Christian faith— in this village a half dozen people. In that, perhaps ten families would become Christian. In a third village two or three families would be baptised. Thus, a half dozen little churches of six to ten families each arose. Wherever this happened, the mission opened a school. It was unthinkable that Christian children should grow up illiterate, thinking of themselves as Untouchables and idolaters. Christianity thus appeared to these few Christians as a religion that gave Satnamis a chance to get their children educated. The teacher was also the pastor of the tiny congregation. He called them to worship once a week, and, when it was convenient, they came.

In one of the villages there lived seven families who had been a robber band. The seven were roughly treated by the police. Because robberies were carried out at night, police would turn up at midnight, knock on the door of each house, and make the man get up and show himself. If the police found the men missing, this was good evidence that they were out robbing. The police required the people to give them rice and other foodstuffs. It was commonly believed that they also forced the women of the robber band to have sexual intercourse with them.

The robbers began to say, "Though we have stopped robbing, we are still persecuted. Let's become Christians. If we have a pastor and a teacher here, the police won't harass us. The missionary will stand up for us."

However, in the twenties, the evangelistic missionary in Bilaspur became deeply involved in erecting an extensive set of buildings for the Burgess Memorial Girls' Boarding School. It was a noted institution in the district. Government officials were pleased at this well-run boarding school for girls. The evangelistic missionary neglected the village schools. They looked like a poor show compared with the prestigious girls' school attended by the daughters of many leading men in Bilaspur. So the movement just described around Bilaspur gradually came to a halt. Only three little sealed-off congregations remained. Such arrested people movements are common in many parts of India.

Evangelisation of Satnamis Reactivated

Then, under the impact of the Mass Movement Survey of 1930-32, launched by the National Christian Council and carried out by the Revd Waskom Pickett, the Indian evangelists and the evangelistic missionaries of the United Christian Missionary Society renewed their interest in the Satnamis. Donald McGavran was then field secretary of the 70-missionary mission in India. Under his leadership the mission decided to put more men and money into the evangelisation of the Satnamis. In 1936 the mission located the McGavrans, my wife and myself, in Chattisgarh, to evangelise the Satnamis and, if possible, begin a Satnami people movement toChrist.

This location I resisted. I was an educational missionary and did not feel evangelism was my gift. While I saw the opportunity and had urged that the mission take this step, I had spent six years, 1924-30, as superintendent of mission schools and director of religious education for the whole mission. I had made some contribution to the educational programme of other missions. I felt that evangelising was not God's will for me. So for three months I resisted this unreasonable location. I told the mission that we would not go to Chattisgarh. I considered leaving the mission and joining some other mission. I said to myself, "If my people think so little of my educational experience and expertise as to put me out into village work, I'll leave this mission. If we go to Chattisgarh, I'll need to learn the village language. All my specialisation in Hindi and my study of Sanscrit will be wasted. This is not God's will for me."

However, I finally yielded. God seemed to be speaking to my missionary comrades. They were sure we ought to go into village evangelism. So my wife and I said, "We'll go there under one condition, namely, that you will put some significant resources into evangelising the Satnamis." The mission felt our proposal was reasonable.

Many seeds sprout, and many seeds perish.

4

Peoplewise Evangelism Begins

The McGavrans Move to Chattisgarh

In April 1936 the McGavran family moved from Jabalpur in north Central Provinces to Mungeli, in the southeast corner of Central Provinces. We moved from a large city of several hundred thousand—on a railway, a divisional headquarters, a university centre—to Mungeli, a small town of perhaps 6,000, 30 miles off the railway in the heart of the great plain of Chattisgarh, a very backward part of India.

We moved into the big old mission bungalow, which George Jackson had built in 1886. Its walls were a foot and a half thick of sun-baked brick. It had high ceilings and a good tile roof. It had a large sitting room, a large dining room, and three bedrooms—each with a small bathroom attached—and ample verandahs. It was a cool, comfortable place built according to the style in which Europeans erected their residences in the latter half of the 19th century.

The People/*Jati* We Found There

As we settled in, our first task was perfectly clear. We had been sent there to carry on a special drive to win the Satnamis to Christ, to start a castewise movement of this specially prepared people, or in universal language a peoplewise movement to Christ. This people thought of itself as a monotheistic section of the population. In theory it had renounced all gods and worshipped only the True Name. In practice, however, it both feared and placated the evil spirits and worshipped the popular

37

Hindu gods. It often gave the names of the gods to its own sons and daughters. It went on pilgrimages to Hindu shrines and had, in fact, slipped back into Hinduism. However, theoretically it was a monotheistic sect. They were True Namers. They were Satnamis. Over the previous 70 years a few thousand of them had become Christians and had prospered.

How does one evangelise a population like this? There were maybe 80,000 Satnamis in the Mungeli subdistrict. Fifteen or twenty miles in all directions from Mungeli extended a well-populated, well-watered plain with villages every half mile or so. Perhaps 70% of the population were Hindus of various castes: Gonds, Kurmis, Rajputs, Brahmins, and others. However, a very large proportion of the population, somewhere between 20% and 30%, were Chungia Chamars who had become Satnamis. They lived sometimes in entirely separate villages. At the head of some of these was a Satnami malguzar or feudal lord. In most cases, however, they lived as outlying sections of villages dominated by the Hindus. They had been counted Untouchables but fiercely resented the name and claimed that they were not Untouchables; they were Satnamis; they were True Namers. The Hindus counted them as a very low segment of the population.

Into this plain, some 50 miles east and west and 40 miles north and south, the Christian Mission had come in the 1880's. From that time until 1936 it carried on, as I have described in previous chapters, much evangelistic work. A Christian community had grown up. This had arisen sometimes by individual converts, sometimes by small groups of converts and sometimes by orphans being picked up and sent to the Damoh orphanage. When orphans graduated after six to ten years of schooling, they came back to Chattisgarh where they had been born. There they either were employed by the mission or found employment in the town. Some of them became teachers in mission schools. The best of them became evangelists—part of the evangelistic team that each station maintained. Some became helpers in the mission hospitals. Some became carpenters and masons and found work either in the mission building programme or in the towns and villages. Some became peasants cultivating a few acres of land.

As our neighbouring mission had done at Bishrampur, the Christian Mission bought two small villages—one at Pendradih nine miles east of Mungeli and one at Fosterpur ten miles west of Mungeli. In these villages to cultivate their acres were settled converted families who could not remain in their ancestral villages. Thus by 1936 there were three strong but small congregations in the Mungeli District—one of 300 members at Mungeli itself, one of 150 members at Pendradih and one of 100 at Fosterpur.

The above account of the formation of the beginning Christian community in one mission could be repeated by scores of missions in many parts of the great nation India. Other beginnings would certainly differ in details. But the process by which small, very slow-growing congregations were established at or near mission stations was typical of many missions in most parts of India. The process was also typical in some other parts of Asia, Africa and Latin America.

Only in areas where a large castewise or tribewise movement to Christ had developed was the process just described radically different. The castewise movements, commonly and erroneously called mass movements in those days, had developed all across India. From the far north to the far south and east to west in a few Untouchable castes and tribes such people movements to Christ had developed. Over 100,000 Churahs had become Christian; 200,000 Madigas became Christian; 200,000 Nagas became Christian; and on and on. While nine-tenths of the Christians in India had become Christians by these people movements, the far more common (and much smaller) result of mission evangelisation was the kind of Christianisation described in this book.

Part of the Christian resource was the remarkable man I have already mentioned, Hira Lal. He had a high standing amongst the Satnami community. He had been very influential in bringing about that meeting at Set Ganga, that mindset amongst the Chungia Chamars that back in 1917 said, "Let's all become Christians." Although that movement failed, he was held in high respect by the Chungia/Satnami aristocracy of this 80,000 Chamar population. Hira Lal was in 1936 a man of 65. His main work was in the hospital, and from this he drew his salary. Because he was at the hospital, many people came to it. They liked Hira Lal. He liked them. Together with his medical work he also carried on an extensive Christian witness.

The other Indian leader of marked Christian influence was the Revd G Samuel. In 1936 he was the pastor of the Pendradih church. He himself cultivated a few acres. He felt at home in any village. He was an ardent evangelist. He often accompanied me and other evangelistic teams when we were evangelising the villages of the plain. Padri Samuel and Dr Hira Lal were the most influential Christian leaders in the Mungeli-Takhatpur areas during the years 1936-54.

The missionary force in Mungeli was made up of Dr Victor Rambo and his wife and two educational missionary ladies, who ran the school and the girls boarding. With the new plan there would now be three evangelistic missionaries: one at Fosterpur, one at Mungeli, and one at a new station to be established north of Mungeli, which was in the fertile plain fringing the Maikal range to the north. The problem was, How shall we develop a programme intended to start a movement to Christ in the Satnami caste of this Mungeli *tahasil*? How does one start a Christward movement amongst 80,000 people? It is to these questions I shall now speak. What was to be the message?

The Gospel and the Christward Movement

Of course, the message must be the gospel. It must be the good news that by belief in Jesus Christ men[6] are saved, and by living according to God's revelation in the Bible men do God's will and are blessed. They come to have new life. Their sins are forgiven. In one bound they are transformed from people of the world into God's people. They have become disciples of Jesus Christ. The development of full-blown Christian character, growing in grace, will take time, particularly amongst an illiterate animistic population.

A great deal has to be done to lay a foundation of firm Christian belief. It is impossible to teach multitudes of illiterate men, women and children to read all at once. Some of them will, with much work, become literate; but most of them, if they are to worship God in a Christian fashion, must while still illiterate memorize sections of Scripture: the Ten Commandments, the

---

[6] Men in this book means men and women.

Lord's Prayer, the 23rd Psalm, the Apostles Creed and other essential Scriptures. These must be used liturgically in their worship. Otherwise they assemble, hear what the pastor says and promptly forget it. But if they have memorized these Scriptures and constantly use them in a liturgy of worship, they are blessed by them. If in addition they know by heart 15 or 20 Christian hymns—set to tunes they already know, of course—then their worship will create Christian minds in them. The message must be the gospel: "Believe on the Lord Jesus Christ and you shall be saved." It must also be couched in their linguistic form and memorized.

How can we get this message understood by people who have never heard it before? How will it become normal and natural to them? How will it come to them as unshakeable truth? How will they—non-Christians—see themselves moving into the Christian faith? That is the problem that confronted us and that confronts every missionary seeking to win a non-Christian population.

There were many answers to these questions. First, it was important that as the village audiences, chiefly groups of Satnamis, heard this message, they understand that we were talking about a castewise movement to Christ. The audiences were assembled haphazardly. Sometimes a crowd would gather at a wide place in the street in the Satnami section of the village. Sometimes a large Satnami landowner would be listening to the message spoken to him in a conversational way, by a missionary sitting in his ample courtyard as his guest. He would say, "This is very interesting. Let me call my Satnami friends."

He would then send out his son or some neighbour, and many Satnamis would come in to hear what their respected leader thought was important. Sometimes at a night meeting a magic lantern would be set up and slides of the life of Jesus projected. The evangelist or the missionary gave a message along with each slide. We would say to them, "What we are talking about is you people as a whole moving to Christian faith. Remember, you were all Chungia Chamars, and then your leaders decided you would give up smoking and the worship of idols and become Satnamis. You would all pay a rupee per household to the guru, gather your followers and comrades and move as a group. That's the way in which you Satnamis now will become followers of Jesus Christ, who is the True Name, who is the only true God, who is God's special representative here on earth. He died for our sins and rose to lead and bless all His followers."

The idea of a movement, not of individuals here and there, but of the people as a whole had to be taught. The gospel had to be seen as that which "we Satnamis" ought to accept, as we accept other things. We never do it individually. We always do it in groups of like-minded people.

This statement must be qualified. It is very rare for a whole people to move at one time, because, after all, the whole people consists of hundreds of small groups of five families, 50 families, 70 families, or whatever. What really happens is that a few of these small groups decide to spread a fever throughout the whole body. They come in, sit in the meeting and listen. Then they go home and, in their own particular segments of population, maybe a half a mile or 20 miles away, say, "We ought to become Christian." In this fashion the intention to become Christian spreads through some parts of some villages. Yes, the first thing was to plant the idea that "becoming Christian is a good thing for us to do. We can do it. We can become Christians while still speaking our own language, still cultivating our fields, still living as we have always lived, still being culturally ourselves. All we have to give up is idolatry and immorality."

In the second place, the gospel had to be presented in the light of Ghasi Das" message. All the Satnamis accepted Ghasi Das as their own prophet. "We are followers of Ghasi Das. He told us to abandon idols and to become True Namers. He said, "Eat no meat. Meat is abhorrent to the True Name'. We gave up meat."

So as we preached the gospel we said, "Your own guru, Ghasi Das, foretold a hundred years ago that there would come a red-faced man with a big hat and a big book in his hand. Well, this is the red-faced man and this is the big book. Listen to what it says. It amplifies what Ghasi Das proclaimed. Remember that he said, 'I don't know what the name of the true God is, but whatever it is, it is the True Name.' This Book tells all men that the name of the True God is the Father. God is our Father. He loves us and sent His Son to save us. Here is the Book that tells everything you need to know in order to be saved."

Thus in many ways we tied the gospel to the message of Ghasi Das, so that it came to them not as an invitation to leave their religion but as an invitation to fulfil their religion. We had an extraordinary opportunity. In most cases, in most lands, the missionary doesn't have this option. In many cases the missionary cannot say, "This is what your own prophet has foretold." In such cases, the advocate never mentions the other religion. He simply proclaims Jesus Christ as God and Saviour and encourages men and women to become His followers.

In the third place, we presented this message as something that groups of them would want to accept. We never said, "If only one of you believes, that is an error or a sin." However, we often said, "When one of you believes, and many of you will, by all means seek to win others of your own people to your faith. Get others to accept the Lord Jesus Christ. Let them tell of their acceptance, not to us but to you, so that you build a group of your own."

One highly intelligent man, long before he spoke to us, went to his own intimates and friends and said, "I'm going to become a Christian. I'm going to be baptised. These are the reasons I'm going to be baptised." After hearing his reasons, they said, "Those are good reasons."

He asked, "Will you join me?" Some said yes, others said no. To those who replied yes, he said, "Pick up a handful of dust, pour it on your head and make Mother Earth your witness that the day I am baptised, you will be baptised with me."

Fifty-seven people, pouring dust on their heads, swore that they would follow him into the Christian faith; however, only nine kept their promise.

The idea we tried to inculcate in all of our evangelism was that those who believe on Jesus Christ **are not leaving** their caste. They are **leading** it out of darkness into light, out of bondage into liberty.

It is easy to say this. It is easy to proclaim this in a village street or the courtyard of some village home. It is difficult, however, for those who believe to put it into practice, because when they are baptised, the rest of the caste will ostracise them. At one place seven families were baptised. When the next morning the women went down to bathe in the river, the rest of their caste people shouted, "Move on down the river. We do not want Christian splashes, your dirty water, to fall on us. If your water falls on us, we shall be defiled. So, move on down."

The Christians had to bathe 20 yards downstream, so their splashes (splashes of another caste) would not defile their former fellows. Ostracism of various sorts was put into effect.

It was—and is—difficult for people to see themselves not as leaving the caste, but as leading it into the light. That may be what **they** think, but in the beginning of any movement the majority of the people in the village, their own people, say, "You are traitors. You have left us. You have gone and joined the Christians."

While we advised and encouraged them to move in groups, we realised that these groups would frequently be squeezed out. Of course, if the group was the majority in the village, then the people who squeezed them out were the minority. Their ostracism did not hurt much. On the contrary, if the converts were a minority, it was difficult to avoid an ostracism that hurt.

In the fourth place, we said to them, "Becoming Christian is primarily a matter of becoming God's people, learning God's Book, gathering **nightly** for worship and instruction, understanding what God requires, and living the life that God has ordained for us. He has described it accurately in the Book. When you become Christians, you will meet every night for worship. We will send you a teacher who will live amongst you. You'll know him intimately, and when you assemble, he'll read God's Word to you. He will teach you God's Ten Commandments. He will teach you to pray the Lord's Prayer. He will teach you the Beatitudes and Christian hymns. You will become a regularly worshipping people. Then as soon as one of you has learned enough Bible to become the leader of the village, we'll take the teacher away. One of you will become the pastor of this group."

We said this, but it didn't have much meaning until we began to get a few small village congregations that **did** assemble every night. Suddenly what we had been saying was understood. They saw it happening. They saw the Christians assembling. They heard women who had been totally ignorant of any religious teaching repeating from memory the Lord's Prayer, the Beatitudes, and the 23rd Psalm. Christians would wake frightened in the middle of the night and say, "I will fear no evil: for thou art with me; thy rod and thy staff they comfort me." Then they would go back to sleep. This fourth emphasis helped to make the Christian faith real. They said to each other, "We can live in God's presence. He is a present help in time of trouble. We can ask Him for healing or for warding off danger. We are God's own people."

In the fifth place, we were explicit that when they became Christians, they must abandon idolatry. We said, "Ghasi Das told you to throw away all idols and you did it for a few years, but now you have slipped back into idolatry. When you become Christians, you must really abandon it permanently. Without the Bible and becoming Christian, however, there is no way you can avoid drifting back into idolatry as you have done. Your educated young men now, in order to earn money, go around and conduct idolatrous services for which you pay. All this is utterly abhorrent to God. When you become Christians, you will give up idol worship. You may go to the great fairs that are held at Hindu sacred places, but you will not worship the gods there. You may go there to sell your goods or to buy other goods. That is quite innocent, but you must not go into the temples and worship the gods. You will also not fear the evil spirits. If an evil spirit troubles you, you will simply command it in the name of Jesus Christ, and it will depart. Jesus Christ has much more power than the evil spirits. "

In ways like this, we sought to develop a way of thinking that would start a castewise movement to Christ of the 80,000 Satnamis in the Mungeli district. Padri Samuel, who frequently made himself a part of the evangelistic team, was a very great aid in developing a Christward movement.

A Practical Difficulty Arises

A considerable problem arose in regard to the placing of the missionary families. In 1936 the McGavrans moved to Mungeli, to the big old bungalow that was vacant at the time. In accordance with its promise, the mission then located the Moodys at Fosterpur, and the Reynolds family to "the Mungeli area." The Reynolds were on furlough and not due back for another year.

The missionary residence problem was this. There was really only one missionary residence, the one at Mungeli into which we had moved. At Fosterpur was a small residence built for Indian staff some 25 years before. It was unsuited for a missionary family, and yet Edgar Moody and his wife bravely said they would be happy to move into it. It was four small rooms in a row, with low ceilings. It was very hot in the summer. It had no septic tank, no toilets, and no fenced yard. Edgar Moody put in a septic tank and toilets. He fenced a yard and planted some trees. While the house itself was never comfortable, it became a possible place in which to live. However, the question as to the third family residence remained unsolved.

It was clear that if we told the Reynolds that the mission was locating them in a new territory where there was no missionary residence, they would probably not accept the location. They would have to live in a hut until they built the bungalow.

Facing this situation, Mrs McGavran and I said, "Very well, let's invite the Reynolds to come and live in the comfortable bungalow in Mungeli, and we will go north 20 miles and rent an Indian house if we can. If we can't, we'll build some kind of a temporary shelter where we can move the family." The problem was helped, to a degree, by the fact that Edgar Moody's family circumstances suddenly required his going home a year early. That left Fosterpur vacant. So, the McGavran family moved out to Fosterpur in 1938 and lived there until May of 1939. The Reynolds family moved into the big bungalow at Mungeli. The plan was that when the Moodys came back, they would go back to Fosterpur, and the McGavran family would move on to the totally unoccupied Lormi Plain to the north of Mungeli.

Dr Hira Lal had long advocated the establishment of a new station there. There were a dozen strong Satnami villages, and their malguzars or feudal lords were friendly to Hira Lal and the Christian cause. Dr Hira Lal had advised me to tour that area during our residence at Mungeli in 1936-37. We had found the Satnami leaders open to the message. They invited us to come in the evening; they assembled their people. They listened cordially. They said, "Yes, we all want to become Christian, and we will think about it." We felt that were a mission station to be established there, and were we able to visit them, not once or twice in a year but once or twice a month, their small interest could be fanned into a considerable flame.

Tragically, while on furlough, Edgar Moody stepped out of his car on the highway into the path of an oncoming motorist, and was killed instantly. Shortly thereafter, the Reynolds decided that they really did not feel called to and would not continue as evangelistic missionaries in the Chattisgarh plain. They wanted to go back to their former station at Kotmi. The mission, seeing that they were not happy at Mungeli and did not intend to work there, moved them back to Kotmi. Mrs McGavran and I were left with the entire district as our field of labour. The plan to concentrate resources there had failed as far as the missionary group was concerned.

In 1939 the McGavrans went on furlough. When they came back in the fall of 1940, they found that in addition to the now empty bungalows at Fosterpur and Mungeli, the mission bungalow at Takhatpur (an important little town between Bilaspur and Mungeli) had become available as a missionary residence. The Revd H C Saum who had carried on the evangelistic work in Takhatpur, reaching the age of retirement, had for the last time gone on furlough. The McGavrans consequently settled in Takhatpur and after 1940 managed the work of the Mungeli-Fosterpur area from there.

Evangelism Proceeds, Victories and Defeats

However, the mission plan had not failed in regard to the Indian staff. Edgar Moody's team of evangelists remained in the district, so that I found myself, not with four Indian evangelist helpers, but with eight. With this large team I was able to cover a substantial part of the plain. Sometimes a couple of evangelists would go out with me. Often two or three teams would go out on their own. Thus the Satnami villages and Satnami sections of other villages heard the gospel many times.

We had victories, and we had defeats. Defeats are always hard to understand. In one village west of Fosterpur, a leading Satnami, a highly intelligent man respected by all of his caste fellows for 20 miles around, decided to become a Christian. He and a group of three families together became Christian. The day he was baptised in his village pond the leading Satnamis from ten miles around assembled to witness the event. After he came up out of the water and put on dry clothes, a number of them said to him, "Don't you ever revert to Satnamism. We're watching you carefully, and if this is good for you, we will all follow you into the Christian faith." That was a high moment. It occurred in early May 1938.

Unfortunately, this notable convert fell ill in the next month June, just as I was about to leave on vacation for the hills. I took him in the car to the Mungeli hospital. Sure that he would get careful medical attention, I went on to the hills. I was terribly dismayed when a telegram reached me four days later saying that he had suddenly died. The damage to the Christian cause was enormous. All those men who had gathered at the village pond to see him baptised now said, "Become a Christian, and the gods get you. Become a Christian, and even if you go to the Christian hospital where, no doubt, they give good treatment, the gods follow you there, and they take your life." The Christian cause had suffered a disastrous defeat.

In a war many battles result in defeat; but the war goes on until victory is won.

5

Starting New Congregations

This book is being written in order that the tremendous effort now being devoted to reaching the unreached peoples in every continent may be of maximum effect. Great danger exists that reaching unreached peoples may be considered simply a matter of **getting Christian messengers there**. These, it is hoped, will then proclaim the gospel. Men and women will hear it and a few individuals will become Christians. The danger is that they will hear the gospel, hear it presented, possibly in contextualized forms, and yet not turn to it. Look at Japan, where only 1.09% of the population in 1982 was Christian.

The error of defining "reaching" an unreached people as merely getting there physically, totally misses the essential meaning of this crucially important first step. This chapter will present a more adequate description of "reaching an unreached people."

Between the missionary—who may be a citizen of that nation—getting there and a people movement to Christ developing lies a complex process. It will differ in details from people to people, from *jati* to *jati*. However, the main steps in this process are similar for most peoples. This chapter will describe the main steps as they were carried out for the Satnami people.

In effective evangelism, or the discipling of any people, a first stage with two steps must be followed by a second stage with six steps. Each step will now be described in some details.

49

Stage One—The Beginning Years

In the first stage, the beginning step is that the gospel be presented in their language and their thought forms—in ways that they can understand.

The second step is the winning of individual converts here and there. Most of these will accept Christ from mixed motives. A rather small percent will come from entirely spiritual motives. A few will have an understanding of the Christian faith sufficiently biblical, and an experience of Christ and the Holy Spirit sufficiently real, that they can tell others of Christ. As they do so they may win a few, or many, or none. One in a thousand may be able to win enough of his or her own people to start a people movement. Of the people movements that are started, many will for one cause or another, be arrested. Successful movements of an *ethnos* are rare.

This book is being produced at a considerable expenditure of time and money, unjustified unless it illuminates the vast territory and describes the many steps that lie between the missionary getting there, learning the language and the culture, and winning the first few individuals to Christ **and** the development of an **effective** evangelism which leads not merely individuals here and there but **segments** of the people to Christ. We are commanded to disciple *panta ta ethne*—all the ethnic units in the world (Romans 16:26). The Great Commission tells us to disciple *panta ta ethne*. In Hindi this reads *sab jatiyan ko chela karo*, "disciple all the castes." That involves the enrolling of ethnic unit after ethnic unit. It involves the beginning, nurturing, perfecting and extending of people movements. This book deals with some of the necessary steps in order that each *ethnos (jati)* may be led to Christ and enrolled. Each should see a stream of its **own** men and women becoming sincere believers and responsible members of churches.

Any attempt to disciple an unreached people must develop a workable programme of effective evangelism that results in many groups of a responsive segment of society following Christ. Stage One of that programme has been described.

Stage Two—Multiplying Small Churches

We now turn to the second main stage of evangelism and set forth its six main steps. These follow the two parts of Stage One just described. These six are the steps by which we in the Takhatpur area groped our way across the vast territory without any previous model. Ours was an exploratory journey. Nobody told us to take these steps. In the course of the years they simply appeared to us as reasonable and effective. These things **could** be done, given the circumstances under which we were then working, and the resources God had given us.

Step One—Searching for a Receptive Segment

The first step is that the evangelistic programme be carried on in a people that has turned somewhat receptive. The Satnami people, (which I have spoken of as if it were **one** segment of India's population) was itself divided into many segments. In this distribution some were resistant and some receptive. There were Jahari Satnamis. These were fundamentalists. These had no idols in their houses and never worshipped idols anywhere. They ate no meat and obeyed all the rules Ghasi Das had laid down. Had they been Christians we would have called them committed biblical Christians.

At the other end of the distribution were those who were Satnamis only in name. They worshipped idols. They had no allegiance to one God. They did not even try to know Satnam. They were bound by some of their caste rules. They did not marry outside their caste. They did what the caste council told them to do. They did not **openly** do those things for which they would be ostracised or driven out of the caste. But they did these things in secret.

For example, while meat eating was strictly forbidden, meat was easy to obtain. Satnamis didn't keep chickens. They would have been ostracised for that because everybody could see they were keeping chickens; but to buy a chicken at night, take it home, secretly cook it and enjoy it, this they could easily do, and many did. In regard to idol worship, very few had idols in their homes; but when they went to a fair, a *mela*, everybody bathed in the tank. As they came out, if they threw water on the stone image of the god as an act of worship, who was to reprove them or throw them out of the caste for this?

In between the Jaharis and the nominals were many other groups of Satnamis.

Amongst these many segments of the population some were quite friendly and some quite hostile. Perhaps someone had gone to the mission hospital and been cured. He had come to think of Christians as friends. When the missionary and his co-workers arrived in his village, this man said, "Yes, these are the people I saw when I was in the hospital. If it hadn't been for them, I would have been dead. So let me welcome them as people to whom I owe a debt." His was a receptive group, possibly in a generally unreceptive village. That was one way in which receptivity arose.

Or somebody read a tract and said, "These Christians are saying something important. Let us listen to them. We're not going to become Christians, of course. We're Satnamis and proud to be, but they may have something good to tell us." That was another way receptivity arose.

A third cause of receptivity might have been that they had relatives who were Christians. "Yes, I know," someone might say. "My second cousins became Christians 30 years ago, and one of their boys is now a medical assistant in the hospital and one a teacher. They're getting good salaries. Becoming Christians seems to be a way up in the world." Such people did not understand the gospel but they were ready to listen to it.

The witness of a rather ordinary Christian, a carpenter by trade, illustrates the point. Once I took him with me when I went preaching in a village. He said that he had relatives there, so I suggested that he come along. The crowd gathered in the village street. As the evening meeting progressed, I said to him, "You've been a Christian for a long time. Do you have anything to say to these people?"

He replied, "I certainly do." He then stood up and said, "Listen, you people. Many of you are my relatives. You know who I am; I know who you are. I heard someone ask what good it does to become a Christian. Let me tell you what good it does. I am an illiterate man, but I have six grown daughters. How many of you have six? Mine all went through the mission school. They all got good jobs. The six of them together are earning nearly a thousand rupees a month. Are any of your **sons** earning a thousand rupees a month? Of course it is good to become Christians. It enormously increases your earning capacity."

That testimony to the value of Christianity is not one that I ever gave or most evangelists would give, but it was effective as a beginning. Many of the Satnamis looked on Christianity as a way up, a way of increasing standing in the community, a way to get ahead in the world. For an oppressed people it was certainly that.

For these and many other reasons, segments of villages were responsive. Other segments were quite hostile. Perhaps somebody had gone to a Christian hospital and died. His relatives and friends would not be particularly open to the gospel. Or there was some Christian whose life had been far less than ideal, who had lied or cheated or reverted to Satnamism, saying that Christianity was no good. Looking at such, some villagers would say, "Yes, some Christians get ahead; so do some Satnamis. But some Christians do not get ahead. No, we're not interested in Christianity."

Whatever the causes might be, certain groups of Satnamis were receptive, and certain were not. We sought out the receptive. We did this in many ways. Let me mention one of them.

We never went to a village for an evangelistic campaign unless we got an invitation from there. If we were preaching and the people said, "This sounds very good," we'd say to them, "Would you like us to bring this team to your village and have a ten-day meeting? You have listened to a **little** of the good news, but if we came to your village for ten days, you would listen to a **great** deal. You would know much more."

"Oh, yes," they'd say, "we'd be pleased to have you."

We would reply, "We'll come on one condition: namely, that you invite us and give us a house to live in. We'll bring our own food, but we'll live in your house. We can't stay out in the open fields. If you really want us, make available a place where we can live."

This was a good test. Few of them had spare rooms in their houses; but many had cow sheds. It was a simple matter for them to say, "We'll tie the cows outside for ten days; it won't hurt them. We'll sweep the cowshed. It's got a roof over it. We'll spread straw on the floor and you can sleep there and cook there."

Whether it was a spare room or a cowshed, if they made available a place for us to stay, we felt their invitation was sincere, and would set a date.

Thus we chose groups to evangelise, in which to try to start churches. We'd try to make two or three villages a month during the dry season, the first of October till the first of May. In some of these evangelistic campaigns the missionary went along. Some of them were conducted by three or four Indian evangelists, with the most experienced in command. Arranging the dates, deciding who was to go where, making sure the invitation was solid, and that it was at a suitable time—all these took considerable planning.

There was no use going to a village during rice harvest. Nobody would come to our meetings. Everybody was working 12 hours a day and coming home dead tired and going straight to bed. But villagers have much spare time when the pressure of the agricultural cycle is light or gives them a few days' leisure.

There was no use going to a village when some great *mela* or fair was taking place in the area. Most of the villagers would stream off to the fair, paying no attention to the evangelistic campaign. Such considerations were part of preparation.

Once a village had been chosen, we'd send a man on cycle to tell our host that we'd be there on such-and-such a day at about ten o'clock in the morning if it were a near village, and three o'clock in the afternoon if we had to walk 15 miles to get there.

Arrived, we would get settled. Sometimes we had to clean the cowshed ourselves or finish the cleaning the housewife had begun. We had to set up cooking arrangements and decide where the team would sleep, where visitors would sit and talk. We would walk around the village and see how it was laid out, where the important people lived, and where the night gathering would be held. After the villagers had eaten supper, the first night meeting was held. Usually a big crowd assembled.

Step Two—Intelligent Gospel Proclamation

The second step was to have clearly in mind how to present the gospel. It was no use preaching a series of eight sermons from eight brief texts. They would listen but would not remember. Sermons that would go well in America were not an effective teaching vehicle in a Satnami village, where most listeners were illiterate.

More than half of the listeners would be women, who thought they couldn't learn. The men would attend and listen but were not likely to respond if we asked them to repeat what we had said. The young people aged 10 to 20 were those most likely to learn and least likely to influence what the villagers did.

The device that we used to present the gospel was to choose ten Bible **stories**. If we had a very brief evangelistic campaign we used only six. If we had a long campaign (ten or twelve days), then there were ten. I use this word "story" intentionally. A story they would understand and eventually learn. It was a series of events. It was what somebody like themselves in villages like theirs did. So they identified with it. They understood it. Furthermore, a story was something that not only the children but also the men and women could learn. It was easy to get the children to repeat the story. It was difficult to get the men to do that. It was very difficult to get the women to repeat anything in public. But once the story took firm hold of their minds, once they understood the events, it could be done.

After the story had been learned, its **teaching** could be drawn from it with ease.

Eight Bible Stories Taught

Eight Bible stories were generally used. The first was of the creation of the world and the fall of man. Then skipping the entire Old Testament we told about Christ's birth. The third story was Christ's curing the leper, His tremendous mercy. Then came the stilling of the storm, His tremendous power. Or that story might be changed to His healing people and casting out evil spirits. Because we were in a population partially animistic, Christ's power to cast out evil spirits and to heal the sick was emphasised.

A fourth story was Christ's forgiving the woman taken in adultery. In Satnami villages, and indeed in the entire Chattisgarh plain, adultery was common. Gonorrhea and syphilis were everywhere. All acknowledged that adultery was wrong. All knew that if caught in it they would be punished by the caste. Nevertheless, practically everybody did it at one time or another. Christ's forgiving the woman taken in adultery and telling her to sin no more spoke to their need. "Your sins can be forgiven," we would say, "provided you, like the woman, believe on Christ and sin no more."

A fifth story was that of Christ's teaching good conduct.

Another story was that of the rich young ruler. Christ demanded that the young ruler leave all and follow Him. Being a Christian was a matter of complete dedication. It was following Jesus Christ wherever He might lead. Nothing was so important as to follow Jesus Christ and to do what He told us to do. "Sell all your goods and give to the poor," He said to the rich young ruler. He does not say that to everyone, but He did to him. When the rich young ruler couldn't bring himself to do it, he turned sadly away and was lost.

Then came the story of the crucifixion. We had to tell this very carefully. If we told the story simply as an event, hearers were likely to say, "Well, the Jews finally caught up with the poor fellow and killed Him." That negated the essential meaning of the crucifixion. So we emphasised that when He was arrested, when He was before Pilate, when they were nailing Him to the cross, He could have said but a word and fire from heaven would have descended and burned up His persecutors. But He didn't destroy them. He forgave them. He said, "Father, forgive them, for they know not what they do." It was a deliberate sacrifice of Himself for the sins of all mankind—for the sins of Americans, for the sins of Indians, for the sins of Jews, for the sins of Satnamis and Brahmins. We would say, "Christ died for **your** sins. But in order to claim such forgiveness **you must believe on Him.**"

Opportunities for teaching were very great. The crucifixion is a most dramatic event. It never failed to hold the attention of the listeners.

The last story was Christ's resurrection and His present rule throughout the world. These eight stories and others were the vehicle on which the gospel was mounted. The plan of the eight-day campaign was to teach one story a day, both in the homes during the afternoon and at the night meeting. We taught it until many knew it well and some could repeat it, and then we set forth the lessons the story contained.

Step Three—Planning the Day's Evangelism

The third step of the programme was a morning study period for the team. The men, who had sometimes been working till twelve o'clock at night, arose about seven in the morning. The people of the village had already gone to work in the fields. Nobody was in the village until about noon, when the women came back from work to bathe and prepare the noon meal. The men would return at one or two o'clock, bathe, eat, and have an hour or two of leisure before going back to the fields.

When the villagers were out working in the morning, the team met to report on the previous day—what kind of reception they had had, who seemed to show special interest. The team met to plan the day—what story to tell, what teachings to emphasise. Then it would spend a half hour in prayer. The men prayed for God's guidance. They prayed for villagers by name. They didn't know the names the first day, but after two days they knew the names of all in the village. Then one of the team was given the task of telling the story to the evening gathering; he went off to prepare his half hour of public address. The songs were chosen, and the day's emphases were laid out.

Step Four—Evangelising House to House

At eleven-thirty the team ate. At twelve o'clock it would sally out. From then till five in the afternoon came the fourth step of the programme—visiting house after house. The village might have 20 or 30 Satnami houses. We would seldom visit the houses of other castes. If the team had three segments, each would have six or eight houses to visit.

A couple of us would go to a house and ask if we could sit down. Most houses had the housewife, the man who had just returned from the field and the children. We would say to the woman, "Go on and cook your meal, while you listen to us." The children would crowd around. The man would settle himself comfortably to listen. So we would get small audiences, sometimes two or three and sometimes ten or fifteen in the courtyard. There we would tell the story for the day. After telling, we would ask some child to repeat the story. We would then tell it again and say, "Come this evening; you'll hear this story and what it means to you in this village."

We'd then go on to the next house. We spent perhaps half an hour in each house. If we got a warm reception, we would stay longer, asking about the family and their relatives. Part of the task was to get to know the people.

In addition to the story we taught God's Ten Commandments. If we were there for ten days, one commandment would be taught each day—both in the houses and in the night meeting. We would say, "This is the command of God: thou shalt have no other gods." That was a good one to start with because it latched onto Satnami teaching. "This is what Guru Ghasi Das told you," we said. "This is what Satnam says. Now we all will say, 'Thou shalt have no other gods.'"

Nobody would speak. We'd say, "Yes, yes, **you** say it. I'll say, 'Thou shalt have,' and you say, 'Thou shalt have.'"

Perhaps a boy would say it and we'd commend him, "Splendid! Now let's do it again. All of you can do what that boy did."

Encouraging them, we would usually get several saying the words after us. Sometimes when they did not say the words out loud, we'd see their lips moving and knew they were repeating the words. The story and the command gave considerable opportunity for teaching.

At five o'clock we would come back to the cowshed where we were staying, prepare and eat the evening meal, and make ready for the night meeting, which was, of course, emphasised in all the house meetings. "We're going to have a great meeting tonight. It will be a most interesting meeting. You will enjoy it. It's going to be in the courtyard of such-and-such a person, or under the big tree. Be sure and be there."

We got promises. They didn't all keep their promises, but we solicited them just the same. The crowd would assemble, understanding very well what was about to happen.

Step Five—The Big Night Meetings

The night meeting was the climax of the day and was the fifth step of the programme. Each night the Bible story of the day was told, taught and repeated. Then the **meaning** of that story was brought out in a half-hour address. Sometimes it had already been brought out in a courtyard to perceptive listeners. Some were so interested that they would say, "Yes, that story has meaning right here in this village." If that had been the response in a house gathering, we were particularly pleased, because we could quote that person in the evening and everyone would be extremely interested.

At every night meeting we'd sing the day's hymn (which had been sung in most of the courtyard meetings) and tell the command of the day and get as many as possible to sing along with us and repeat the command after us.

After the meeting there would be conversations with specially interested individuals. We tried to teach them enough so that on the closing day they could retell the Bible stories, so that a fair number of them would have memorized the Ten Commandments. We'd tell them on the first day of the campaign, "Before we leave, many of you will know God's Ten Commandments. What a wonderful thing!! What a privilege for you to know what the eternal God has commanded. We would not tell these commands if they were merely our commands."

We would open the Hindi Bible, a big, impressive volume. We would name the book, the chapter and the verse. We would implore everyone to listen. Then we would read the impressive commands. The goal was to teach them enough so that they could tell other people. We hoped they would say, "Yes, this is really God's Book. We ought to have it."

We would encourage them to tell other people. "Learn this command (or story) so that when you visit your relatives or when you wives go to your mother's home in other villages, you can tell this story of God's love for us to your loved ones. Tell of the Lord Jesus' mercy in curing the man suffering from leprosy. Tell of His demand of the rich young ruler. Tell of His death for us on the cross. Spread the good tidings that through faith in Jesus Christ your sins can be forgiven and you can become saved men and women. That's what we are. We are real Satnamis because we have the Book. We intend to obey Satnam and do what His Book tells us to."

In this kind of evangelism we had two main goals. The first was to teach them enough so that they would retain what they had heard—not forget it in five minutes.

One time walking through a village, I saw a young man threshing his rice. When peasants thresh any grain, they erect a pole in the middle of the threshing floor and cover the floor with sheaves from the field. They then tie six or eight cattle together with ropes around their necks and drive the line of cattle around and around the pole. As the cattle walk over the sheaves, their hooves tread out the grain. After the cattle have gone around and around the pole for hours, the peasant rakes off the straw. There on the earth is the precious grain. He sweeps that up and stores it in his house. That is his life.

This young man, driving the cattle round and round, was singing one of the hymns we had taught. He kept singing loudly, "King Jesus came, King Jesus came. To save poor sinners, King Jesus came." In the case of that young man, we had achieved our first goal of teaching the people biblical truths, Bible stories, the facts they needed to know about the life of Christ and the purposes of God. The decision to follow Christ and be baptised might be made later on, but knowing biblical truths was the first step in anyone's becoming Christian. The entire programme was built around the learning of biblical truths, followed—we hoped—by intelligent decisions to follow Christ. The young man at the threshing floor had taken the first step.

The second goal was to lead some of them, hopefully all of them, to become open committed followers of Jesus Christ, baptised members of His Church. As the evangelistic campaign progressed, excitement mounted. Some one of the co-workers would say, "One of the men last night took me aside and we talked for two hours. This man is deeply touched. He really wants to become a Christian but is terribly afraid that when he is baptised he will be thrown out. So I told him to get four or five other families. Many of his friends in the village will want to believe with him. In this fashion I encouraged him. He is not an influential man. I'm not sure how resolute he is. Let us pray for him."

Other team members would tell of other possible believers. The names were never made public because this would subject these inquirers to severe persecution. But they were encouraged to speak to their friends. Sometimes a group would be formed. Many times it would not be. In ten evangelistic campaigns if one group would actually declare for Christ, be baptised and form a church, we felt God's power had been wonderfully displayed.

Step Six—Forming New Christian Groups

The sixth step was the formation of a Christian group, a beginning church. Those who thought of becoming Christian were moved by various motives: desire for health, desire for social advancement and love of Christ. Some would say, "We never heard teaching like this before. He must be the Saviour, because there is nobody like Him." A motive like this we treasured but did not see often.

One of my fellow workers was named Yishu Charan—the Feet of Jesus. This is a Hindu form of name. Many Hindus are called Ram Charan—the Feet of Ram. So my friend's parents had named him Yishu Charan, the Feet of Jesus.

He was a good preacher, a fine singer. He and I late one night talked with the strongest man of the village, who could bring everyone else in the Satnami community behind him. He sometimes led them in evil ways. He sometimes led them on an armed raid against another village—a very secret affair. Had it become known, they would have been arrested and put in prison by the police. This strong man manifested a considerable interest in becoming Christian and leading the Satnamis of his village to become Christians. "We'll all become Christian," he said.

Yishu Charan and I met him out behind his haystacks after the night meeting broke up at ten o'clock. We talked till two in the morning, but we were not able to bring him to firm decision. At two o'clock we finally concluded that he was not quite ready.

Three Important Questions

In every case where groups wanted to become Christian three important questions had to be answered. The first of these dealt with economic difficulties.

How to Deal With Economic Difficulties

Many peasants of the plain of practically all the castes borrowed money in order to continue their cultivation. Perhaps an ox would die and they'd have to buy another but didn't have the cash. Perhaps they needed money to get a son married. They'd go to the money lender and borrow money saying, "We'll pay this back at harvest time." He'd lend the money at 70% a year interest, and they hoped to pay it at harvest time.

If the harvest was poor, the debt would not be paid. The money lender would say, "Never mind, pay it next year. You'll have a good harvest then," and the interest would mount. These loans were always secured by mortgaging one's land. If the loan was not repaid, the money lender was by law given the land. Since many of the loans were not repaid, the money lenders became owners of much land. This they would hire peasants to cultivate on a system called *adhiya*. The peasant would give half the seed grain; the owner would give the other half. The peasant would do all the work. When he reaped the harvest, he would give half the grain to the money lender and keep half for himself. The peasant almost never got his land back.

As a result, a great deal of the land of the Satnamis had been filched from them, and money lenders had become rich. Many of them became malguzars who bought villages with the profits of lending money. Peasant landowners became landless labourers working for the landed money lenders.

When a man became a Christian, the Hindu money lender reacted. He didn't like the idea of one of his dependents, one of the puppets he manipulated, whose land he would sooner or later seize, becoming a Christian. "This man," he said to himself, "has passed out of my control."

So he would say, "Bring me the money you owe me. I need it right now. If you don't bring it immediately, I'm going to foreclose the mortgage. I was kind to you through the years, but I can not be kind any more. Bring the money."

The man would be up against a tough problem. If he didn't pay immediately, his land would be gone.

All over India land is exceedingly precious. There is only so much of it. There are more people than there is land. It is treasured. It is difficult to buy. Peasants will say, "I may die, my son may die, but my field must not die. It must be sown and cared for. It is the only source of life."

As we evangelised these indebted people, we faced this tough problem. If we said to them, "We have nothing to do with your economic life," then when they became Christians, many would lose their land immediately. If a man became a Christian and lost his precious land, that effectively debarred him from becoming a Christian.

On the other hand, if we said to them, "Very well, here is the money. What you owe to the money lender you now owe to us. Go and pay him off and pay us at harvest time," then another tough problem faced us. Then becoming a Christian seemed to be a monetary transaction.

Consequently, as peasants came to us who had borrowed money and said, "When we become Christians, our money lender will immediately demand repayment," we had to study such people very carefully. "How much land do you own? Do you pay your debts? Can you pay your debts?" We would reach a thorough understanding of the man's economic condition. If he was a careless fellow, who probably would not pay his debt, we had to say to him, "Become a Christian, but your land is already gone. We will not lend you money."

If on the other hand, he was an industrious man, had paid his debts in the past and was likely to do so in the future, then we would say to him,, "We will not take your field as security. Bring us gold earrings or silver bangles or armlets or anklets or some other security that we can keep so that if you do not pay us we will be able to recover the loan. Then we will loan you the money."

We helped many peasants; but we feared the loan fund led some to become Christians chiefly for monetary reasons.

All helpful social action involves this danger. Feeding the hungry, curing the sick, educating the ignorant, fighting for justice—these are good things to do. But if they are followed by men and women becoming Christian, then, at least sometimes, people are becoming Christian for non-spiritual reasons.

Where one person alone becomes a Christian, the danger of his doing so for some social reason is acute. Where a people movement develops and dozens, scores, hundreds or even thousands become Christian, the danger is very much less.

When to Baptise

Another most important question in enrolling ethnic units is whether converts should be baptised immediately or after much teaching. Our practice was to investigate carefully those who desired to become Christians. We were in a village for eight or ten days. If a group was becoming Christian, we lengthened our stay to two weeks or more. We found out a great deal about prospective converts from their neighbours and the village feudal lord. The converts knew we would not baptise them unless they knew the Ten Commandments, the eight stories—especially that of the crucifixion—and a hymn or two. Prospective converts also had to pledge to assemble nightly for worship. A successful campaign would climax with the baptism of the three, four, five or more families.

I pause here to record the different practices of different denominations and missions facing different circumstances. Many would not baptise inquirers for a year after they had declared for Christ. If during that year they attended worship regularly, learned regularly, and lived good Christian lives, then they would be baptised. The resident worker would teach them; the superintendent on his annual tour would baptise them. That is a sound procedure. However, it seldom takes place at the beginning of a castewise movement to Christ.

To be remembered, however, is that unless a strong people movement is going on, unless the pressure to follow Christ is great, that baptismal practice is likely to stop a movement rather than to encourage it. Other evangelists would baptise at the drop of a hat. A famous Methodist missionary carried a bottle of water with him. As he preached, if anyone said, "I believe in Jesus Christ," he would stop right there, open his bottle, pour out a handful of water and sprinkle the man in the name of the Father, Son and Holy Spirit. He would then say, "You are now a Christian, a baptised man; your sins are forgiven; live like a Christian. Get others to follow Christ. Form a church. Walk to the nearest church to worship. You are now one of God's chosen people." In the hands of that missionary, facing his particular circumstances, that system worked well. The Methodists at that place had a growing Christward movement.

Other missions would follow a method between these two extremes. Some like us, baptised after a week or ten days' instruction and investigation. Some baptised at the end of the first month or the first three months or when the missionary next visited that village. Various practices were followed. All effective evangelism must answer this question as to when to baptise. The goal is an ongoing responsible cluster of churches.

How best to get that cluster is the essential question. When do you baptise? Is baptism the sign to everybody that these of our caste have really decided to follow Christ? Or is it a rite administered by the missionary or district superintendent to those who have proved that they **are** Christians?

Our practice was to baptise at the end of the evangelistic campaign. Instruction, ceaseless conversation and local investigation had gone on for many days. We knew the groups well. Some we refused, some we accepted. Some we advised, "Wait. Persuade your relatives. Tell others of the Saviour. You have made a good beginning. You three families now talking about becoming Christian are ready to be baptised. You can win six or eight more. It will be far better for you to be baptised with ten families than with three." Our decision varied with the circumstances.

How to Provide Adequate Shepherding

The next move in the formation of a Christian community was forming the baptised into a living church. The converts had made the great move. They had declared, "We are no longer idolaters. We are Christians. We form a separate group. We love our relatives. We trust that they will also follow Jesus and come out of darkness into light." The converts had made the first move toward becoming an ongoing church.

Our policy was to insist that the group be shepherded from the very beginning. The history of the previous 80 years in Chattisgarh, the experience of the Evangelical Mission, the General Conference Mennonite Mission, the American Mennonite Mission, the Methodist Mission, the Pentecostals, and ourselves all indicated that to baptise a group and then leave it, sending a preacher there perhaps once a week or once a month, was futile. Most of the converts remained Christian for six months or a year or two, and then they reverted, paid a big fine and were readmitted to their old caste. They then said, "We tried Christianity and it didn't work."

Some converts in the previous 80 years had remained Christian. For the most part these were those who moved into Christian settlements at or near a mission station. Such Christians had placed a great distance between themselves and normal Satnami peasants. We were convinced that to disciple an *ethnos*, a caste, many ongoing churches had to be established **in normal village communities**. Assembling scores of individual converts at central stations was not going to achieve that end.

Consequently, we resolved that whenever a number of families committed themselves to Christ, we would send a teacher who would stay with them, know them intimately, live in their midst, assemble them—and hopefully some of their neighbours—every night for learning and worship. Before baptism they had pledged to gather five nights a week and on Sunday. Every night would be a teaching session and a worship experience.

This programme enabled us to have at the end of the year a well indoctrinated congregation. Its members would know twelve Bible stories by heart and could tell them. They would know the Ten Commandments, the Lord's Prayer, the Apostles Creed, the 23rd Psalm, and ten hymns. They would have a new self-image and begin to think of themselves as men and women who really know God. "As Satnamis we did not know Him; now we know God."

Mungia Bai was a good friend of mine. I said to her, "What's the difference between you now and you who 20 years ago lived as a Satnami?"

She replied, "In those days, when the gurus or other important men came to our house, my husband would say, 'Don't show your face around here. This is a men's meeting.' Now when you come, they say, 'The women must come to learn. You women are God's daughters, just like men are God's sons. You want to learn God's Word.'"

That kind of a mind was formed by our discipling programme. That, we believed, is the base of any soundly Christian Church. Such men and women know they are God's people and intend to follow God's instructions in the Bible.

Paid Pastors

Leaving a teacher in every new congregation involved an economic decision. Who would pay the teacher? The group of five or six families? Quite impossible. The group of eight or ten families? Again quite impossible. Had we had 40 or 50 families, they could have paid their village pastor. But the beginning groups we were getting—small groups of four to ten families— could not. Yet if they were not instructed, if they did not have a resident teacher, the likelihood of their reverting was great. So we placed a teacher in each little congregation **at mission expense.** Sometimes the converts would provide a house for him. Sometimes we would rent a house from one of the believers. An unbeliever would never rent us a house. Sometimes we had to purchase a small piece of land and build a mudwalled, two-roomed house. Such houses could then be built for about fifty dollars or 150 rupees.

The teacher and his wife moved to the village and lived in that house. That gave the new congregation a good Christian family, husband and wife, both literate, both practising Christians, both having spent two years at Bible school. They would soon come to know every member of the Christian community and most of the remaining Satnamis, too. This system insured close contacts with all members of the new church. Despite these arrangements a few reversions occurred; but most converts remained Christian. When the movement was arrested in 1947, the village churches continued on even though they were clearly isolated outposts of the Christian faith. The rush to the cities—urbanisation—damaged them. Their best young people streamed off to the cities in ever-increasing numbers. In the long run, the rule "grow or die" will likely prove its validity.

A firm, thoroughly biblical foundation is essential in all propagation of the gospel.

6

Creating Effective Pastors

The considered attempt between 1936 and 1954 to reach an unreached people, that is, to start the discipling of the Satnamis of Chattisgarh, was a long, complex undertaking. This chapter will describe the **system of pastoral care** of groups of new Christians.

By way of introduction, let us recall the three stages that all reaching of the unreached necessarily involves. These three stages are: 1) proclaiming Christ as divine and only Saviour; 2) encouraging men and women to become His disciples; and 3) transforming new Christians into responsible members of His Church. This chapter describes the third activity or stage; but to understand it, we shall look once again at the mindset of the *ethnos* (*jati*) being invited to accept Christ as Saviour and Lord.

The Mindset of the Listeners

As evangelisation begins, one must assume that those being evangelised are ignorant of the Christian message, resistance to which is likely to be high. Christianity will be considered a new religion challenging the old. It will be considered untrue. Its listeners will suppose that advocates are paid to convert them and it is their business to resist such persuasion. Sometimes political or even military considerations weigh against any acceptance of the new faith.

This was the Satnami mindset in the Mungeli district between 1883 and 1890, when George Jackson, the first Christian missionary in the area, toured the villages. He preached the gospel, was heard with curiosity, and won only a few to Christ. He was followed by my father, John McGavran, in 1892-93. He also toured widely, sold Hindi Gospels and tracts and explored the field. This was the beginning of the seed-sowing era. Between 1893 and 1936 several other missionaries evangelised the Mungeli-Bilaspur villages. All encountered this same mindset.

My experience between 1933 and 1936 in Jabalpur, the headquarters of our mission, illustrates Stages One and Two. I was then field secretary for the India Mission of the Disciples of Christ. My work was heavy; nevertheless, I gave an evening a week to evangelising what I considered to be a responsive caste, namely, the Dumars. While a few were employed by missionaries and other Christians as sweepers in their homes, no Dumar had ever become a Christian. A few had sat in Bible classes conducted by missionaries but had not become Christians.

Two or three Indian companions helped carry on this weekly attempt to win Dumars to Christ. In two and a half years we used many methods. None was successful. All presentations of the gospel were listened to with interest but did not win open acceptance of Jesus Christ and willingness to be baptised and become members of the Christian community. Only in the third year did four families become Christian and thus start a small movement to Christ that brought in about 50 families of Dumars before it stopped.

To be sure, in this earliest stage of all evangelisation, the exploratory stage, when opposition or indifference is high, when ignorance is being diminished and acquaintance established, a few souls here and there turn to Christ, as Hira Lal of Mungeli did in 1888. But for the most part, converts are not won, and if they are, they are likely to come one by one.

In this early stage, converts are so fiercely persecuted or their faith is so weak that they sometimes backslide. In many places the proclaiming activity lasts for years. In some—alas—it is not followed by multiplication of congregations for perhaps 100 years or more.

During the second stage small groups of men and women of a responsive caste are won. A man believes the gospel and brings his wife, his brother and his wife and some nearby neighbours. Several families of the responsive *ethnos* become Christian. Sometimes they come for spiritual motives; sometimes they come because they have quarrelled with their own people and are already somewhat separated. Such rebels often listen to the gospel readily. Their willingness to follow Jesus is helped by their feeling of estrangement and perhaps even hostility to their caste fellows. Motives are always mixed. Even the most spiritual motive has social or other facets. These may be hidden but are nevertheless there. Whatever the motives, during Stage Two, groups are won. Once a group is won to Christ and baptised, the third stage begins. Small groups must be transformed into ongoing congregations.

Unless a pastor is placed in a village to shepherd the new congregation, the following is likely to happen. The team that won the converts leaves the village saying, "We'll be back next Sunday. Be sure and gather for worship." For some time Sunday worship continues to be led by a worker from the outside. The visits diminish to once a month and then to once in several months, depending on circumstances, weather, floods, and the work at the central town and other villages.

Small groups of Christians in the villages are often subject to counter-persuasion and even persecution. Their neighbours and friends say, "You became Christian. What good did it do you? You still have to work just as hard as you ever did. You still get sick. Your child who was sick died just like ours do. Becoming a Christian hasn't done you any good at all. When you want to get your son married, none of us will give you a daughter-in-law. All told, you had better come back to us."

Until a strong people movement to Christ is born, this counter-persuasion, couched in many different forms, goes on all the time. After a people movement grows strong, such counter-persuasion grows less and less effective.

As a result, when between 1860 and 1936 (76 years in which no strong people movement had been born) Christian groups were established in Chattisgarh, by our mission and neighbouring missions (Mennonites, Evangelical, Methodists, and others), there were many reversions. Responsible members of village churches were not often seen. Consequently, my labours in Chattisgarh were dominated by the conviction that multitudes of churches, one in every village, each with many responsible members, were necessary. Establishing them was God's will and my task. The third stage I am heading toward in these beginning paragraphs was clear in my mind. Though backsliding had often happened, it must now be overcome both by **more converts** and **much better shepherding.**

Pickett's *Christian Mass Movements in India* had convinced me that castewise movements to Christ had occurred and would occur. A movement among the Satnami caste was possible. God had sent me to bring one about. I devoted myself singlemindedly to that task. I was working for the establishment of many churches—congregations of reasonably knowledgeable believers, resolved to remain Christians and to win their caste fellows to Christ. New Christians should believe in Christ; they should also believe that as Christ came to seek and save the lost, so they themselves were to seek and save the lost—their fellow caste people, brothers and sisters, uncles and aunts, in-laws and distant relatives. All these were lost until they believed on Jesus Christ. It was the privilege of the new Christian to win them.

Proclaiming Christ, described in the preceding chapter, was a necessary first part of the programme. **It should be followed by year after year of systematic biblical instruction.**

Biblical Curriculum for Beginning Congregations

After groups were won, adequate pastoral care had to be provided. It was not sufficient to have a campaign, bring believers to decision, and baptise them. What was required in addition was regular worship, systematic learning of God's Word, reproof of evil and encouragement of good conduct. The teachings of the ten-day campaign were a good beginning. If we were to go away and leave the new, largely illiterate Christians who had no habits of regular learning and worship, what they had learned during the campaign would very soon be forgotten. Furthermore, pastoral care in successful people movements all over India was convincing proof that such care could be provided. It had been provided by Baptists, Presbyterians, Methodists and Lutherans. Adequate biblical instruction could be provided by us.

I was particularly impressed by the nightly learning and worship carried on by Episcopalians in South India. There the pastor living in the village would gather the Christians together in the church **every evening** for a half hour of learning and liturgical worship. They became responsible members of Christ's Church.

I constructed a three-year curriculum of Bible lessons and memory passages to be taught by the pastors to the members of their churches. The first year required teaching the Ten Commandments, the ten Bible stories, five hymns, the Lord's Prayer, the Apostles Creed and the 23rd Psalm. The second year there were other sections of Scripture, other hymns, other accounts from the Old and New Testaments. The third year there were still others.

In order to encourage this, we printed a series of beautiful certificates. A green certificate was given to those who passed their examination at the end of the first year, a red one for those who passed their examination at the end of the second, and an impressive gold one for third-year graduates. All certificates were printed on cardboard—about 8 by 11 inches in size—and when won were tacked up in the homes of Christians. This system of pastoral care and biblical instruction was put into operation. Regular learning and worship, singing of hymns, audible repetition of biblical passages and prayers in nightly worship, soon gave the Christians a sense of being God's people.

I now repeat a sentence from the first paragraph of this section of Chapter VI. "What was required in addition was regular worship, systematic learning of God's Word, reproof of evil and encouragement of good conduct." Please note that regular worship heads this list of desirable learnings. Men and women who become Christians must have a vivid sense of God's presence. They must love Him. They must feel assured of His power. When they call on Him, He will answer them. When they wake up frightened in the middle of the night, they will repeat to themselves that notable sentence in the 23rd Psalm: "Though I walk through the valley of the shadow of death, I will fear no evil: for thou art with me; thy rod and thy staff they comfort me." Then they will quietly go back to sleep. Christians are now God's people. He will look after them.

To make such worship natural they must become accustomed to daily worship. They must assemble every night for worship led by one of their own people or by the village pastor. That unfortunate custom all over the world whereby Christians worship God only once in seven days and then when led by a paid pastor must not be allowed to develop. Christians must worship God every day. They must commit to memory not only the Lord's Prayer but other passages of Scripture and must use these liturgically every evening, so that when they are alone or meeting as a family group they can quote these memorized passages and be assured of God's presence and power. They are now God's people, and He is a very present help in time of trouble. Becoming Christian must mean becoming men and women accustomed to worship God, thank Him and praise Him.

Creating Village Pastors

A serious problem facing us was, Where can we get the pastors who will do all this? It's easy enough to plan it in the safety of a parsonage or mission bungalow and put it down on paper, but how does one carry it out day by day and night by night in villages where this has never been done before? There was no nearby pattern of this sort.

A great deal is written today about the desirability of indigenous forms of worship. Missionaries are cautioned about **not** imposing Western forms. Much of this is ivory tower talk, by arm-chair theorists. There are no indigenous forms of congregational worship. There has been no infallible Bible to be memorized by men and women, boys and girls alike. Worship has been the placation of evil spirits.

Any meaningful biblical worship will be new and strange. However, we must not overstate the case. In Chattisgarh all Christian worship had to be in their language with people sitting on the floor, men on one side and women on the other. Most tunes were local and all explanations of the Bible were in the thought forms of the villagers.

Congregational worship was new, but gradually this new worship became thoroughly **theirs**. Their non-Christian friends who attended felt quite at home and understood perfectly.

In 1936 the churches were at the mission stations. The people who worshipped there were literate Christians. They had been reared in orphanages, or having lived on or near a mission compound for many years had learned to read and write. Many of them in the 1930's and 1940's were second and third-generation Christians. Furthermore, the missionaries also worshipped at the mission station churches, and their presence and the presence of a pastor and other church and mission workers guaranteed that at each central station there was a devout band of **literate** Christians. They used hymn books and brought and read their own Bibles.

But this was not a feasible pattern in the nearby villages where almost everybody was illiterate. Peasants of the plain were not accustomed to congregational worship. Practically none of them had ever been to school for a day and certainly not to a Christian boarding school.

Consequently, the question arose: Where do we get pastors who will shepherd and teach new small congregations of illiterate men and women? The first answer was, We'll get them from the evangelists now evangelising. In this area work eight evangelists who carry on campaigns in many villages. They preach the gospel at night, they go from house to house teaching the Ten Commandments and the ten Bible stories. They get to know thousands of Satnamis. When a group decides to become Christian, one of the evangelists becomes the village pastor.

The next question was, How big must the group be before we give it the full-time services of a pastor? It would be very nice to win 100 families, but that never happened in the Mungeli District. Or even 50, but that never happened. Or even 25, but that never happened. We were getting groups of four to eight families. Facing that situation we made a rule that we would never place a pastor unless there were four families who had become Christian. When four or more families became Christian, we put a pastor there.

It was easy to say, it was difficult to do. These evangelists for the most part were famine orphans who had grown up in an orphanage; they were accustomed to secure life and the company of other Christians. They spoke standard Hindi, not the local dialect. They were literate. They had the security of a mission compound with the presence of a missionary who loved them and cared for them.

When I said to them, "Leave this Christian community and go live in a village," they would reply, "You are telling us to do something very difficult. There we will be the only Christians of experience. There we'll be living in the midst of strange, low-caste people. We'll have to conform to village patterns. We will have to obey the village feudal lord. We men may be able to do all this, but our wives will feel frightened. Our children will grow up with children who are not Christian and whose ways of life do not appeal to us at all."

Such words expressed the resistance to location in a village, that we encountered as we sought to recruit from the evangelistic team pastors for these new village churches. Sometimes the evangelists would flatly refuse. In fact, I had to say to one evangelist—a good friend of mine—"If you do not accept a location here, I shall have to transfer you to another station. Work in Takhatpur involves your not only winning converts but establishing ongoing churches. Establishing a church means living in a village with your family and over several years developing a really Christian community."

Fortunately, we had three on the team who were local men. They had been sent off to mission schools for six or eight years. So they had both the advantages of being seasoned Christians, literate and well educated, and of being villagers. They made good pastors if they once agreed to live in the villages.

We soon found a second source for village pastors—the best of the new converts. A few of them were slightly literate, and they fitted very nicely into the village situation. However, there were some substantial difficulties in the way of that solution. First, most of the new converts were almost illiterate. Even the few who knew how to read had learned it in school years ago and had almost forgotten it. They were not accustomed to reading. The best of the older men also, who had passed the age of 40, had trouble reading at all. Their aging eyes were not that good. Furthermore, they had grown up in villages where a low sexual standard prevailed, and sexual laxities of one sort or another were common. Men thought nothing of proposing to women a hidden casual sexual alliance. Furthermore, their standard in money matters was not high. Borrowing money was easy; paying it back was difficult. Getting money for one reason and using it for another was common.

For example, I appointed one man, whose pre-Christian name was Khor-bahara (Street Sweepings). His parents' previous children had died, taken by evil spirits, they believed. So when this boy was born, they called him Street Sweepings, so that as they called him by name the listening evil spirit would say to himself, "I don't want street sweepings," and would pass him by. When he became a Christian, we changed his name to David. David was an able man and became one of our village pastors.

He was living in a rented house and the owner of the house said to us, "We won't be able to rent this to you much longer." Our only option seemed to be to buy a piece of land and build a house on it.

David came to me and said, "A good plot is available for 200 rupees. Give me the money and I'll bring in the deed next week."

Next week, however, he did not bring it in. About six or eight weeks later I said to him, "Hey, where is the deed? What has happened?"

He said, "As a matter of fact, I found a two-acre field that I bought for my own use. It will give me enough rice to eat the whole year long, and I will pay this money back gradually. I took it as a loan."

It is that kind of carelessness and even dishonesty in regard to money matters that a new convert may sometimes display. Villagers were also men who had grown up never doing anything systematically. They had not gone to school regularly. They did what they wanted. To them, nightly worship or nightly instruction of any sort was unnecessary. Most of these men had no regularity in their bones. They had no watches and time was always approximate.

However, the great advantages of using villagers as pastors were constantly before me. They knew the people very well. They liked village life. To them, living in the villages was no problem. They had many relatives with whom they were on intimate terms. Often they were highly intelligent men. Had they had the opportunity, they would have been college graduates. I found them cheerful and willing. It was a pleasure to work with them as colleagues. The village pastors also frequently served on the team of evangelists. When they were absent from their villages, their wives led the nightly meetings.

We appointed two of the best of the new converts. Tularam was one of these—a highly intelligent man. He had a first-class mind, a friendly disposition, and a genial way. He was liked by everybody. When he became a member of our team, his conversations and presentations of the gospel were notable. He made an excellent village pastor.

The third source of village pastors was the ablest of the young illiterate peasants. These had to be trained. They were owners of an acre or more of land, men of some substance who, as they became Christian, showed a genuine faith and interest in the Word and in learning.

One named Avadh owned ten acres of land and was a bright young fellow. He had a remarkable mother who was baptised with him. She was a highly intelligent woman, full of common sense and a great deal of Christian devotion. After the baptismal service, while sitting in Avadh's house, I said to him, "Avadh, have you ever seen your name written?"

He said, "No, I never have."

I said, "Well, here it is." I wrote the three letters in Hindi script, which in Roman script are A—V—DH.

He looked at it and said, "Well, I've never seen that before."

I asked, "Why don't you write it?"

"Oh," he replied, "I couldn't possibly do that. I don't know how to read or write."

I laughed, "Of course you can do it. Here, give me your hand."

I took his hand, put the pencil into it, and just underneath the letters I had written, I traced A—V—DH, again, of course, in Hindi script.

"There," I announced. "You have written your own name with your own hand." He looked at it in amazement.

Then I said, "Now write it without my hand on yours. You can do it."

He took the pencil and scrawled the various strokes necessary to make those three letters. Giving him the piece of paper I said, "Avadh, you are going to learn to read and write. You will become an educated man because you are now a Christian. You are a child of God. You can do it."

Later he became one of our best village pastors. When I was in India 30 years later in 1971, I heard him preach a thoroughly biblical sermon. He had not only learned to read and write, but had read the New Testament often enough and remembered enough that his sermon was full of biblical illustrations.

Placing village pastors meant getting them places to live— parsonages. This was not easy, because practically all the village residential area was heavily restricted. Fields could not be bought and houses built on them. In the beginning a few times a Christian would provide a house for the pastor to live in. The wealthiest man we ever baptised named Rangia owned 20 acres of land. He wanted a pastor and said, "This house I built for my brother who died. The pastor can live in this house." So Pastor Daniel lived there and did very good work.

Once in a while we were able to rent a house, but that was not usual. The Christians generally didn't have an extra house to rent, and no non-Christian would rent his house to us. So eventually in all places where we had a little congregation we had to buy a plot of land and on it build a house. Since houses were built with mud walls, and hand-made tiles were laid over cheap rafters and bamboos brought down from the forest, such houses cost us maybe fifty dollars each in those days. Putting up a house which was then owned by the mission was a good solution. The pastor had a small garden in which he could grow vegetables in the rainy season. He would make a fence of thorns and sometimes of mud around it. By his very living pattern he became part of the people he served.

Again and again we went through the process just described in getting adequate pastoral care for the small groups of new Christians that the evangelistic campaign brought in. Had this not been done, the groups would have disappeared.

All carrying out of the Great Commission and discipling of ethnic units must multiply ongoing churches and create good pastors of new congregations. Nothing but ongoing churches will fulfil the command of Christ to disciple *panta ta ethne.*

The result was that by 1947 there were 15 small congregations, each with a resident village pastor who lived in the house owned by the mission and carried on regular pastoral and evangelistic work. He had taught the congregation and led it in worship five times a week and on Sunday. As a result, we had firm congregations. These were believing Christians, accustomed to worship regularly in a liturgical fashion. They had gained some knowledge of God and had considerable experience of the Holy Spirit. They had—for illiterates—commendable knowledge of the Bible. All this placed a distance between them and their unconverted caste fellows.

Furthermore, practically all the Christian children had been sent on to boarding school after they finished the village schools. These children were more firmly Christian than their parents. They were more removed from the village community. They had a far better chance of gaining profitable employment and being regarded as educated Indians. These children meant a great deal to their fathers and mothers, who were proud of them. They said, "As our children get educated, merely having educated children lifts our status in the world. We have become somebody. We are no longer the scum of the earth."

Aiming at Self-Support

As soon as possible, as soon as many local Christians are won, their churches should be aiming at self-support. Where large numbers become Christians by conviction **and** are men and women of some substance accustomed to responsible action, pastors will get all of their support from the local people. However, where a poverty-stricken population is being won, a population of landless labourers, or one not accustomed to responsible action, the establishment of an adequate, competent and self-supporting pastoring system is difficult.

Most of the great younger Churches (denominations) of Asia, Africa and Latin America have been started on mission money. Let me repeat that. Most of the great Protestant denominations of Asia, Africa, and Latin America have been started on mission money. In Africa, however, there are some notable instances of tribal turnings to Christ where local pastors were supported by the new congregation. That today in many areas of the world mission money is no longer necessary must not obscure the fact that historically most congregations have in the beginning been shepherded by nationals paid from abroad. This continued until the new struggling Christian community achieved a size and solidity that enabled self-support to become an ordinary way of life. Then, the self-support pattern being seen by surrounding non-Christians and an ever-increasing number of converts, self-support was easily reproduced in new congregations.

The end sought by missions and by missionaries of any race, language, or colour is always a completely self-supporting church. This self-support exists at five levels. The first level is that of the local congregation. The congregation supports the pastor, provides his complete income. The second level is that of the supervisors. Every 10 to 15 churches requires a supervisor who will see to it that the problems of local congregations are solved, the mistakes of a pastor are not inflicted on the congregation for too long, and pastors are changed as needed. At the second level the supervisor is paid by the cluster of churches. The third level of self-support is that required to maintain a district superintendent or bishop of 100 or more congregations. Local congregations contribute funds to pay a district area superintendent, who may be in any one congregation only once a year or less.

The fourth level of self-support is that required to maintain a Bible school or seminary. Pastors need to be trained. Unless training is paid for by the national Church, the Church is not really independent. A great many seminaries and Bible schools around the world today are still substantially supported from abroad. Their buildings are paid for from abroad, their principals come to England, Scandinavia or America to raise money for building programmes, professors' salaries and endowments. Most Churches (denominations) in Asia, Africa and Latin America have not yet achieved self-support on the fourth level.

The fifth level is the missionary societies organised by Third World denominations. On these five levels, self-support is the ultimate goal.

Let us in the light of these goals observe what was achieved in Chattisgarh. The general picture outlined below for the Bilaspur-Mungeli District was also true of the small village churches started by all the other missions.

In regard to self-support, in the Mungeli-Takhatpur District we were stuck at level one. Most of the pastors in the small village congregations were paid with mission money. The pastors got an average of 40 rupees a month. For ten pastors, the mission spent 400 rupees a month, or 4,800 rupees a year which was in 1936 about $1,600.

Most mission works—hospitals, schools, leprosy homes, agricultural demonstration centres and the like—cost at least that much a year and usually much more. Paying these village pastors was easy for the supporting churches in America. Consequently, village pastors were paid by the mission until 1968. I had retired from the field in 1954, so what is said about the situation after 1954 tells of what was done by my successors. Till 1968, the system went on, and the village churches were well looked after. Their children graduated from the mission boarding schools. This rural Christian community of about 900 souls was a part of the smaller younger Church of 8,000 souls established by the India Mission of the Disciples of Christ between 1882 and 1968. The town congregations were self-supporting. Their village churches were not.

In 1968, the executives of the United Christian Missionary Society in America felt the time had come for all the congregations established by the India Mission to become completely self-supporting. They said, "This system of caring for yourselves in a spiritual fashion **only** if the care is paid for from America must stop. It is iniquitous." With one stroke, all salaries of the village pastors were cut off. This was done as a correct moral move, as something that simply had to be done. In effect the mission said to the village churches, "Sink or swim. We hope you will remain Christians; but you will get no more mission money."

What happened? There were no reversions. Christian villagers remained Christian; but Bible study and regular worship almost ceased. Then there was grave neglect. None of the still largely illiterate local peasantry leaped into the breach. They did not say, "We will assemble regularly whether we have a paid pastor or not."

Most pastors continued to live in those villages, forming a disgruntled segment of the congregation. They felt they had been ill-treated, that salary was their right. They asked, "Were not principals of mission schools still paid? Were not doctors in charge of Christian hospitals and leprosy homes still paid? Were not missionaries still paid? Why then should village pastors not be paid?"

Untouchable Responsiveness Wanes

In order to understand what happened between 1936 and 1954, it is necessary to recount the facts that all over India the responsiveness of the Untouchables sharply diminished in the later 1940's. In earlier decades, becoming Christian had seemed to Untouchables as one way out of the sanctified racism that is the caste system. "When we become Christians," Untouchables said, "our children get educated. Some of them at least graduate from primary school, some even from middle schools and high schools, and a few from college." While the spiritual motives for becoming Christians were always emphasised, the economic and social advantages played a significant part.

In the 1940's, however, Gandhi and the upper caste Hindu leaders of India saw clearly that unless Hindus were to offer Untouchables real political power, they would likely all become Christians or Muslims. Hindus would lose millions of votes. Hindus would no longer be the dominant rulers of the vast subcontinent.

The great Dr BR Ambedkar in the late 1920's and 1930's had been proclaiming, "Untouchables must leave Hinduism. Untouchables must become Christians or Muslims. Untouchables must renounce the position of powerless serfs. Untouchables are going to form a distinct voting block entirely separate from the Hindus."

At this point Mahatma Gandhi, sensing a tremendous defeat for Hinduism, declared that he would fast to the death unless Ambedkar changed his position and resolved to lead the 80 million Untouchables to remain in the Hindu voting block.

For more than two weeks as Gandhi grew weaker and weaker Ambedkar steadfastly maintained his position, declaring, "We Untouchables are going to leave Hinduism. We are going to form a separate voting block as India becomes self-governing."

Then the Hindu leadership began offering Ambedkar all kinds of political advantages: "We will guarantee that Untouchables are assured seats in the provincial and national assemblies. We will guarantee that they get more seats than their numbers warrant. We will give you all kinds of political and social advantages. But you must remain Hindus for us to do this."

In the end, Ambedkar was forced to capitulate. The upper caste Hindus used every tactic to blackmail Ambedkar including the threat to murder Untouchables in villages if Gandhi were to die. It is this threat that forced him to sign the Poona Pact. The Untouchables remained part of the Hindu voting block. They got more seats in the legislative assemblies than their numbers warranted. The Poona Pact bound Untouchables to Hinduism. It seemed to all Untouchables that the way to social advance now lay in remaining solidly Hindu. Naturally, with this all-India movement going on and with the Satnami Chamars of Chattisgarh now being assured four seats in the provincial legislative assembly (more than their numbers entitled them to), the Satnamis soon decided that it was politically and economically much more advantageous to remain Hindus than to become Christians. Consequently, the readiness to hear the gospel, believe the gospel, and become Christians sharply declined. As a result, the small churches of six to ten families remained small churches. In the late 1940's and early 1950's there were very few conversions to Christianity. A significant change of mind had swept over all Untouchables, now called Scheduled Castes. Untouchable movements to Christ, not only in Chattisgarh but in all India, substantially slowed or more often stopped.

In the last two decades of the 20th century it is becoming increasingly clear to Untouchables that remaining Hindus has not really changed their status very much. They are still the bottommost castes in the Indian social system. They are still landless, oppressed, and often illiterate. Their leaders are increasingly coming to believe that their only real redemption is to renounce a religion that announces in all its scriptures that the Shudras (inferiors) were created from the feet of God and that their proper duty is humbly to serve the upper castes (see Bhagavad-Gita, Chapter 18).

The above brief paragraphs are an inadequate description of the position now held by 150 million former Untouchables, now called Scheduled Castes and Tribes. But they do indicate some of the climate in which the gospel must be proclaimed in India. It is my firm conviction that nothing can stop the 150 million Dalits (Fallen, Scheduled Castes) from seeking a way out and up. I firmly believe that for them to become Bible-believing Christians filled with the Holy Spirit will be the best way for them to achieve the position that God intends for them.

A Critical Appraisal of the Programme

In 1988, I recount what happened between 1936 and 1954. I ask myself, "What would I do differently if I were back in 1936? Knowing what I know now about the growth of self-supporting churches and being able to correct whatever mistakes I then made, what would I do differently? What should have been done had we been endowed with supernatural wisdom in 1936?"

I mention four points. First, the basic problem was that there were not enough Christians. The United Presbyterians in the Punjab found in 1910 that a self-supporting congregation needed 100 Christian **families**. In most of our villages lived less than ten. There simply were not enough Christians to support a paid pastor in every village. A self-supporting cluster of congregations requires hundreds of adult members, and we had only tens.

Second, the only possible procedure would have been for the strong churches at the mission stations, where there were some hundreds of Christians, to share their pastor. These churches might have said to their pastors, "We will pay you and will **require** that part of your work be the supervision of these village churches. You will conduct the morning service in the town church, but every Sunday evening you will be out in a village church. Caring for these village congregations, scattered from three miles to 15 miles away, is your responsibility. They are our brothers and sisters. We are all one great congregation."

Had any one congregation said that and had its educated town pastor walked out many miles each Sunday, rain or shine, that might have worked. The financial base of the large congregations at the centre was big enough. The town Christians did support their pastors. But they did not say and probably could not say: "All these small village congregations are our responsibility. We will send our pastor to shepherd them. Often he will go out during the week also to meet some need."

This was never said. Perhaps it could not have been. Between town and village was a wide cultural gap. The town pastors would have said that going out every week, rain or shine, was impossible. It may not have been impossible; but it was certainly most difficult. At any rate, it was **not** done.

Third, were I back at the beginning, facing this situation and knowing what I know now, I would stress much more the training of **unpaid village elders**. I mentioned earlier that we did this in a small way. This was part of the plan of action followed for a couple of years. During the rainy season is a six-week break between the sowing and the weeding. At this time agricultural work in the villages is slack, so we brought a half-

dozen of the ablest young peasants to Takhatpur to our Rainy
Season School, gave them food to eat, and taught them to share
in leading their congregations.

After two years we stopped that programme because the
village Christian leaders, seeing that such training did not lead to
paid employment, became uninterested. Possibly we could have
found ways to motivate them, but the conviction that all mission
work was paid for and ought to be paid for was very strong.

Despite this difficulty, were I back at the beginning, I would
stress much more the training of **unpaid lay leaders—elders.**
This was certainly the New Testament pattern. I would do very
much more to motivate **voluntary** leadership. It is easy to say
that now. But in 1942, after no one turned up at the Rainy
Season School, that approach did not seem possible.

Such men would probably have not carried out the careful
teaching and shepherding done by paid village pastors. These
were controlled by the mission, followed a curriculum of Bible
lessons, gave examinations and handed out certificates to those
who passed. They kept the village Christians at a high level of
expectation. They walked to Takhatpur once a month for a day-
long pastors' meeting. All this would not have been possible by
unpaid, slightly literate village leaders. Consequently, we would
have risked major reversions. Whether these little congregations
could have survived with village leaders with no financial reason
for working is an open question.

Fourth, the adequate pastoral care I am describing in this
chapter must include constant growth in numbers of Christians.
Biblical teaching and devout worship of a few must not be
substituted for growth. Discipling an *ethnos* (caste), commanded
by our Lord, certainly means an annual membership obtained by
a steady flow of converts from the non-Christians, adequate
knowledge of the Bible and the habit of regular worship of God.
**It must mean continual winning of the lost of that people to
saving faith in Christ. The winnable must be won while they
are winnable and in large numbers.** The goal, to establish
large clusters of 50-100-family congregations, should be held
constantly in mind by the missionary and his colleagues.
Whether that missionary is Asian, African, European or
American is a matter of no importance.

As we seek to win the world for Christ, anything we do short of establishing multitudes of soundly biblical churches of many families each is defeat. Perhaps it would be better to call it **very slight gain**. Nevertheless, we must hold firmly in mind that despite difficulties, we aim to enroll whole peoples—*ethne, jatiyan*, segments of society. That is what eternal God commands us to do (Romans 16:26).

If that is to be done, each people (*ethnos, jati*) must have enough Christians in it to form numerous clusters of sound, ongoing congregations. For an ongoing Christward movement to form, each congregation in it must have many families and be adequately pastored. To be a sound, ongoing church there must be many families in each congregation and each congregation must be adequately pastored. In New Testament congregations this was done by unpaid elders, *episcopoi*. Each congregation must receive much biblical teaching and engage in regular devout worship. Adequate care by unpaid *episcopoi*[7] or paid pastors is essential.

Discipling an *ethnos*, a people, a segment of society requires continuous labour to multiply soundly Christian leaders.

---

[7]As the churches spread across Palestine, Asia Minor, Greece, and Italy, the New Testament is perfectly clear that most elders were unpaid. Only one passage (1 Timothy 5:17-18) indicates that in the later stages a few elders were paid.

7

Four Stages of Christianisation

This chapter sets forth four stages in the process of Christianisation which the mission was carrying on in Chattisgarh. A similar process should go on as any unreached people is evangelised and discipled. Were this book merely an account of what one missionary did between 1936 and 1954, it would be of little importance. But if this account of one missionary is seen as typical of what missionaries and pastors in many other places do and ought to do as they attempt to carry out Christ's command voiced in the Great Commission, it will be found valuable.

To be sure, in most populations at the beginning of the process of evangelisation, there will not be a great famine. The Christian community will not consist very largely of men and women who came to Christ as famine orphans. That is obvious; but the evangelisation of any *ethnos* seriously undertaken is likely to pass through the four stages or periods I am about to describe.

Those working in Jordan, Lebanon, Morocco, Japan and other highly resistant populations may well proclaim for decades without starting any Christward movement in some section of that population. This may be because the entire population is very hostile to Christ. It may arise because receptive segments of that population may not have been found. It may occur because the missionaries are using less than effective methods. They are depending on education, medicine or indirect evangelism. They are going to the most hostile segments of the population. The Christianity they present sounds to the listeners as a distinctly foreign religion. It is not presented in a way that invites men and women to become Christians within their own cultures.

All these possibilities will occur to those working in resistant populations. And all to some extent were true in Chattisgarh 1936-54. Nevertheless, because of the faith Ghasi Das had proclaimed ("Let's leave idolatry") and because of the great social and economic progress made by those few who had become Christians, these Satnamis and Chungias were not highly resistant. Given the right circumstances, a Christward movement could develop. At least that was what my Indian and missionary colleagues believed.

The four stages of Christianisation now to be described will be carried out by missionaries in segment after segment of the world's population as they turn from indifference or hostility to friendliness to the gospel.

First, there will be a period of exploration. Second, will come a period of much evangelisation and a few converts. Third, will come more converts, and enduring churches of these converts will be founded. Fourth, a time will come, if God wills, when men and women will flood in. Congregations will multiply. It is during this fourth stage when the processes of education, Christian nurture, and biblical instruction should be multiplied, or the church will grow up illiterate, materialistic, people of the flesh rather than people of the Spirit.

We of the 20th century have become accustomed to stories of the planned conquest of difficulties. The discoverer of streptomycin, for example, the big post-penicillin advance, knew what kind of drug he wanted. He set out to get it. He encountered many difficulties, some of them foreseen. He thought and fought his way through these difficulties. Similarly the discoverer of any new product knows what he wants and plans to get it. The stories of how these plans are carried out make fascinating reading.

In much the same way, looking at church growth from the human point of view, the missionary societies organised by Churches in all six continents—Asia as well as Europe, Africa as well as North America—are going about the business of multiplying new congregations. They know what they want— vigourous, thoroughly indigenous, thoroughly biblical, Holy Spirit-filled churches. Commanded by both the Bible and the Holy Spirit they set out to get them. They are confident that Almighty God will direct and control the whole operation.

But that is just the beginning. They encounter all kinds of difficulties that war against the establishment of even a single cluster of congregations. How these national leaders and missionaries painstakingly work through many experiments, meeting many failures for every success, makes a fascinating story.

One short story in the epic of church growth around the world is that in which God gave me the privilege of playing a part. It concerns the India Mission of the American Christian Churches. Our goal was clear: the establishment of vigourous, Spirit-filled Indian churches, growing and thriving in the midst of Indian society. That end was kept clearly in mind by the missionaries. The goal was for me a guiding star through each of the four stages.

Stage One—Exploration

When the pioneers came to India in the 1880's and started their work in the Central Provinces, there were no Christians at all in the unreached districts to which God sent them. The task in each district was to establish a church made up of Indian people. The missionaries preached, taught and healed. In the earliest stage—the exploratory one—they themselves and their helpers comprised the entire church; but they were foreigners and at best spoke Hindi as foreigners do. They lived in a different fashion from the people of the land.

We remember Dives shouting across the great gulf to Father Abraham. Whenever a missionary tries to convey a spiritual message to people of an alien tongue and culture he shouts across a great gulf.

Nevertheless, God granted the early missionaries a few converts. These were ruthlessly ostracised by their Hindu caste fellows. The Hindu religion and its rigid caste system is a system of legitimized and sanctified race prejudice. It was—and is—Christianity that stresses brotherhood. The few converts who dribbled in one by one necessarily joined the existing churches made up of friendly foreigners and displaced Indians—converts from several different castes. It was as if a congregation in America were made up of a few converts from a dozen different minorities—Mexicans, Chinese, Indians blacks and others. All evangelisation during the first stage is exploratory.

Stage Two—Conglomerate Churches

Evangelisation in 1895 proceeded to Stage Two. What with a few converts and some Indian Christian colleagues who were imported from other areas of India where the Church had been established in previous generations, each mission station gradually came to have a congregation made up quite largely of the employees of the American Mission. With the exception of the missionary himself, it was a brown church, speaking the Hindi language and living as most other Indians did. Its members resided on or near the mission compound. It lacked intimate contacts with any of the castes of the land. The grown-up orphans who had come in during the early years of Stage Two did not know which caste their parents had belonged to. The converts had all been ruthlessly ostracised. The town churches were—from the caste point of view—congregations of a new conglomerate low caste—Christians.

Practically none of the non-Christians had relatives amongst the Christians. To put it vividly, Christian preachers could not walk into a dozen villages and kiss women (sisters, aunts, grandmothers of their own) with affection. They had no sisters, cousins, aunts, or grandmothers in those villages. To everyone they were outsiders.

In 1895, Stage Two began and lasted until about 1910. In the first three years of this stage there came a great famine. Hundreds of children were saved from starvation by the mission. For years the principal energies of the India Mission were taken up by caring for orphan boys and girls. Out of them came a limited number of very able men and women and considerable numbers of those with average ability. All were thoroughly Christian, in the sense that they had never known any other religion but Christianity. They were tightly welded together by bonds of common calamity and from five to fifteen years of education and Christian fellowship and worship in well-run orphanages.

The coming of these young men and women into the Christian community strengthened it a great deal. Their coming partly rectified the handicaps of an employee church, lack of connection with the general public and the exclusiveness of the entire community living on the mission compound. Many of them found jobs outside the mission.

Furthermore, in some areas some of the orphans knew some relatives and maintained contact with them. This was particularly true in the Mungeli-Takhatpur area. Many Satnamis knew that the "boy or girl we had given up for dead was saved by the mission and is now a well known teacher or carpenter."

It was a peculiar thing that the more educated and Christian a group of orphans became, the less grew the contact with their non-Christian relatives. The areas in which ex-orphans retained a considerable degree of contact were exactly those where they were given a lesser degree of education. Those orphans who grew highly educated, cultured and Christian were the ones who grew so far away from their humble village relatives that they became ashamed of them, lost track of them, were foreigners to them, could not put up with the crudities and superstitions of their Satnami uncles, aunts, cousins and more distant relatives. So, to a certain degree, the mission defeated its own ends by doing the very best it could for the orphans. It lifted them, to be sure, but it lifted them out of contact with their relatives and thus broke the channel of friendly intercourse through which Christian convictions are spread.

Stage Three—More Converts, Small Village Churches

During Stage Three (1910-36), the missionaries were preaching and teaching Christ. Their Indian colleagues were bearing their own witness to Christ even though separated by great social gulfs from their near neighbours. As a result, here and there across the Mungeli-Takhatpur District a few small groups became Christian. A family or two from this village or from that were baptised. They were encouraged to walk in several miles on Sundays to the mission station church to worship.

Times of need brought in more families. This was because to non-Christian minds, the great advantages of becoming a Christian appeared to be that men and women were helped in times of hunger, sickness, loss of land or other difficult situations.

A man who could not get justice anywhere else had gotten it through the Christians. A woman whose ten children had died within the first year of life got a living child after treatment in the Christian hospital. A person afflicted with leprosy was cared for tenderly in a leprosy home. Who on earth could do these impossible things except Christ?

But pressure to revert to Satnamism was also high. When two or three families became Christian in a distant village, they continued to live there in sickness and health. The thousand and one contacts with Satnami neighbours continued. The preacher, an ex-orphan or an Indian from some other part of India, came in now and then to lead them in worship. But the daily contacts were long-time Satnami relatives and friends.

As a result, there was extensive backsliding. Illiterate people could not get enough Christianity in occasional meetings of worship to hold them through the storms. Pastors living in the central stations were out of touch with the day-by-day life of their village Christians. With very few exceptions, the pastors did not like the life of the village. They who had been reared in a clean orphanage did not like the village dirt. They did not thrive on drinking the water of the pond, in which everyone bathed and washed his clothes. The coarse language of the villager was just what they did not want their children to hear. The lack of medical and educational facilities in the village appalled them. They might go out once a month; but they did not intend to live there. The village was a place where children died suddenly with a high fever, or cholera took a tenth of the inhabitants. Pastors in orphanages or on mission stations would not willingly stay in villages. They wanted to get back to the central station.

Before 1936, many of the hopeful beginning congregations were lost. The converts by virtue of their illiteracy and the religious life of Hinduism were only rudimentary Christians. Some new congregations were formed. Of these, many reverted to Satnamism. The Christian cause lost many of those groups won between 1895 and 1910.

Stage Four—Village Churches Multiply

Stage Four began in 1936 with the Takhatpur-Bilaspur-Mungeli experiment. It was decided to do three things: a) to put a pastor with every four or more Christian families, b) to require the illiterate believers to memorize essential Bible passages, and c) to institute as the Christian way of life, evening worship five times a week in addition to Sunday worship, also usually in the evenings. These three steps would enable converts to become genuine practising Christians.

We also decided to help a few of the ablest villagers to become pastors. These would remain in close contact with their people. These men liked to drink pond water. They loved the village smells and were not too offended at the rough talk. Most of them cultivated an acre or more of their own land.

We intended to conserve every one of the promising beginnings of church growth. We intended to help the new Christians grow in grace, to adjust to their ideas of what was fitting, to learn their dialect, to worship with them in their home dialect and to translate the Gospels into it. We also purposed to understand and sympathise with their economic problems and to educate their children. This last had been an impossibility for these people before they became Christians. Untouchable children were not permitted to enter the schools run by the high castes. But now education of their children opened the door to a different kind of life. All these fruits of Christianity helped elevate the mindset of the depressed classes.

The education of the children instituted an unforeseen difficulty. The ex-orphanage men and women had learned to value education highly. For their children we had opened boarding schools. These residential schools required parents to pay a reasonable fee for each child admitted. The fee was calculated at one-half the monthly per-capita income. Thus, if a man and a wife had eight children, there were ten people in that family. If the family earned 30 rupees per month, the per-capita income was three rupees. The school fee, therefore, was one and a half rupees.

The system worked beautifully with salaried people. But peasant Christians had no tradition of education and did not value it. They did not want to send their children to boarding schools. Their children too, much preferred the free, undisciplined life of the village and the wide-open fields. Further, it was difficult to determine the per-capita income of a man who seldom saw any cash, and more difficult to get him to contribute one-half of that every month for the education of his boy. The mission had to start where it had begun with the victims of the great famine—that is, full support in school—until the thirst for education had been established.

With this approach to the growing church opportunity, results gradually became apparent. Groups that became Christian were likely to remain Christian. The best of the ex-orphanage preachers settled into village life, though with a bit of groaning. Pastors from among the village Christians were developed. Each group of new Christians was led by a resident pastor to worship God, not once a week but five nights a week and on Sunday, averaging 22 times a month. This implanted the truths of the faith even in illiterate minds, even in women's minds. The teaching depended largely on rote memory. This method gives each one who learns a sense of accomplishment and a real comprehension of the essentials. Rote memory is despised in American education, but it is a valuable tool when teaching illiterates.

Backsliders—and there were some of these—were looked upon as likely to repent and become a fruitful source of future accessions to the church. Each new group was a beachhead into the Satnami caste. The church that lives happily in the village is in close contact with the people. Its members have many non-Christian relatives and close neighbours.

In the Bilaspur District and in the Jabalpur urban area among the Dumars, this new approach resulted in small growth of the church. Congregations arose living miles away from a mission compound, in their ancestral surroundings. We learned that congregations that are properly shepherded, really taught biblical truths and regularly led in worship become firm Christians, even if the men and women who become Christ's followers remain illiterate.

However, in 1954, complete self-support was still far away. Thus the search for a thoroughly Indian, Spirit-filled, growing, self-supporting church went on. In 1954 we could say that the end had not been achieved. The small number of people concerned in the Fourth Stage, less than a thousand, did not give the Christward movement a large enough base.

The new church, the rural church, the one-caste church, must grow much more if it is to multiply. It must educate its boys and girls; but it must not educate them so thoroughly that they move away and leave their parents and their non-Christian relatives hopelessly mired in the mud. It must be cared for, but not too much. It must grow in numbers, but it must also grow in spirituality. It must be helped economically and medically, but it must grow increasingly aware that the real treasures of life are spiritual. Christians must believe that God is real and answers prayer.

Thus our mission worked patiently ahead developing churches God could bless and that, we hoped, would grow vigorously in the Satnami soil of Chattisgarh. That purpose dominated the work. It guided my thinking. It controlled my expenditures. I wish that I could say that this purpose guided everything I did; but that would not be true. I was a typical missionary who always lives in the midst of many demands, opportunities and circumstances to which he reacts. I was no exception. Consequently, many times while the discipling purpose was there in my mind, I did something else!

For example, in 1943, when the Japanese were about to invade India and an allied army was rushed into Chattisgarh, many Takhatpur area villages in late May were ordered to evacuate their homes.

"Get out! This 49-square-mile block is going to be made into an artillery range. We need your land right away."

In two weeks all the peasants left. The villages were empty, the fields unsown. For the next six months a great share of my work, expenditure, thinking and praying was taking care of the evacuee Christians. At that time, had we had enough money to offer non-Christian evacuees financial assistance and accommodation, as I provided the Christians, very great growth would have occurred. By non-Christian evacuees, of course, I mean those Satnamis who were close relatives and neighbours of the Christians belonging to the same caste and **already friendly to the Christian faith.** Such non-Christian neighbours of Christian cultivators, if offered help, would have moved into Christian evacuee camps and would have been helped by Christians, where Bible teaching and worship were carried on every night and the sick received good medical attention. Many would have become Christians. But we did not have the money. Consequently, that was a time in which the overall purpose I have been describing was not achieved.

During the years 1936-54 our goal remained clear. It was five-fold: 1) to start a Satnami movement to Christ; 2) to encourage the coming in of groups of 20, 30 or 40 families; 3) to train the best of the converts to be village pastors; 4) to give every man, woman and child enough Christian teaching so that he would become an intelligent believer in Christ; and 5) thus to start many soundly Christian churches. Four parts of the goal were achieved; but since number two was not, since only 17 small groups became Christian, a large ongoing people movement did not occur.

Radical Change of Conditions

The four stages of Christianisation just described are reasonably accurate in regard to much Christianisation in many lands. However, they must always be applied to the real situation. In India today the real situation of the depressed classes has changed very considerably. The last part of this chapter will therefore be devoted to a careful description of the new world in which the Scheduled Castes and Tribes in India find themselves.

The climate changed. Under Gandhi's leadership the Hindus paid great attention to the Satnamis and other depressed castes. Gandhi was afraid that if they did not give them this attention they would become Christians or Muslims. And they probably would have. So Hindus gave them many special privileges. For example, they paid substantial fees for any depressed caste boy or girl who cared to go on to school. They gave them more legislators in the provincial and national assemblies than their numbers entitled them to have. Such considerations made the Satnamis feel that their progress lay not in becoming Christians but in remaining Hindus and taking advantage of these opportunities.

Forty years later, in the last two decades of the 20th century, they are beginning to see that while the privileges offered them to remain Hindus did benefit them slightly, remaining Hindus also fastened the caste system onto them. Hinduism teaches that the Brahmins, Kshatriyas and Vaishyas are high caste; they are the twice-borns. The depressed castes are and will remain Shudras—inferiors. Furthermore, Hinduism, with its theology of karma and transmigration, teaches that the low status of the Shudras was earned. Evil deeds in human lives were correctly and inevitably followed by birth into a low Shudra caste. Hinduism offers no forgiveness of sins, no eternal life, no just, loving and Almighty Father, no Saviour, and no universal Church.

Consequently, Satnamis remain today bound by Hindu convictions that Satnamis are justly and properly low caste.

As long as this mindset continues, their real salvation cannot happen. Among Satnamis today recognition of the bondage of Hinduism is just beginning. All over India such recognition occurs only here and there. In 1981 it led some 10,000 depressed classes men and women in the southern tip of India to become Muslims. Such thinking will gradually lead at least 100 million to listen to the good news of the religion of brotherhood and justice. Great movements to Christ lie ahead. They wait to be born.

The depressed classes of India (the Harijans or Scheduled Castes) are now and for the foreseeable future will be people who can hear the gospel. They are being cultivated and given limited special privileges by the Hindus. This point deserves elaboration.

Their sons and daughters are given scholarships to get them through high school and even college. They are appointed to good positions in government offices. They are elected to state and national legislatures. Some of them are appointed to minor executive positions. With all this, however, real authority is not given to them. Were it given, they would soon dominate the Indian political and economic system. Their cause is very well illustrated by a magazine published in Bangalore, called *Dalit Voice*,[8] the voice of the fallen. This bi-monthly insists that all Scheduled Caste men and women should become either Christians, Muslims or Buddhists. They must not under any circumstances remain Hindus.

When they become Christians today, the privileges given them by the Hindu elite are promptly taken away. If a young Scheduled Caste man with a high school or college scholarship becomes a Christian, the scholarship is promptly taken away. If a Christian of a Scheduled Caste wishes to obtain a scholarship, all he has to do is to renounce Christianity and become a Hindu. He promptly receives a scholarship. In short, if he acknowledges

---

[8]*Dalit Voice* is edited by the noted V T Rajshekar and is published in English in Bangalore, South India.

that he is a member of the lowest caste (the slaves) in the Hindu social system, he will become a well treated slave.

However, we may be sure that in modern India slaves will not remain slaves. The Church in the future will grow from amongst the oppressed peoples. It was an oppressed people that God called out of Egypt. It was an oppressed people that He brought back from the exile. And in the time of our Lord, it was from the oppressed—the common people—that His followers chiefly came. Eleven of His twelve apostles were Galileans and were counted "ignorant and unlearned men" by the Pharisees and Sadducees (Acts 4:13).

The common people heard Him gladly. So in Chattisgarh (and all other parts of the world) it is probably from those who suffer some physical or social disability that the most ardent response to the gospel will come. Physical and social sufferings do not make people Christians, but they do incline them to listen to the good news.

Soundly Christian congregations will also multiply among the favored segments of the population. The time will come when "let's leave idolatry" will be voiced by awakened groups of Brahmins, Kshatriyas, Vaishyas, and others. The gospel is for all men, regardless of their wealth and position.

In the next chapter I shall speak about the tension between service, social justice and carrying out the Great Commission. We shall see the principles involved in that tension becoming real as they are applied. We see them best when they walk before us in flesh and blood. The years at Takhatpur gave me many opportunities to live out the tensions between service, social justice and evangelism.

"For consider your calling, brethren, that there were not many wise according to the flesh, not many mighty, not many noble; but God has chosen the foolish things of the world to shame the wise, and God has chosen the weak things of the world to shame the things which are strong, and the base things of the world and the despised, God has chosen, the things that are not, that He might nullify the things that are" (1 Corinthians 1:26-28, New American Standard Bible).

8

Social Justice and Evangelism

Economic Bondage

Those turning to Christ were the oppressed. They were the Achchhut, the Untouchables, the Satnamis. In the years between 1700 and 1870, in jungle-encircled Chattisgarh these had been fairly large land owners. The landless Chamars had come down from the Gangetic Valley, cut the forest, and suffered the dangers and privations of a pioneer territory. They had made themselves land owners.

But as the British rule swept over the land and law and order became common, Hindu money lenders also came down from the northern provinces. They had money in their pockets. They loaned money to the Chamars and required as security that the Chamars, or the Satnam mortgage their land. "You're borrowing a hundred rupees? Write me five acres of land as security. If you don't pay back the hundred, with 75% interest, I'll get the land."

The Satnami, quite unaccustomed to this kind of dealing, replied cheerfully, "Certainly. With one good crop I'll be able to pay you back." He gladly put his thumbprint on the document, walking many miles into Bilaspur to do it. The binding legal document was then registered. The Satnami peasant had the money; the money lender had the mortgage.

The peasant, who was unaccustomed to paying back money or, indeed, carrying out any of his promises, did not pay back the money. A year went by, and now, with the 75% interest, instead of owing 100 rupees, he owed 175 rupees.

"Never mind," he said to himself, "I'll pay it off next year." The second year he had a 300-rupee debt. In a few years he was due to pay 700 rupees. He could not possibly do that. So, reluctantly but inevitably he surrendered five acres of land.

In 1936 this process had been going on for many decades. Land had been draining away from this Satnami community. When I got there, a great many of the peasants were reduced to one or two acres. A few had three or four acres. A still smaller number had 10 to 15 acres, and only a handful had 40-100 acres.

To a few of those who had lost their land or had mortgaged it at 75% interest per year, Christ was seen as the Saviour, the Powerful Redeemer, the Liberator from the clutches of the money lender. Spiritual redemption was quite naturally eclipsed by economic redemption.

The situation was complicated by the fact that if a peasant, securely in the money lender's power, became a Christian, the Hindu would call him and say bluntly, "Your debt is long overdue. Pay it at once, or I'll foreclose."

The money lender could—and did—make "becoming a Christian" mean "losing my land." Even if the man turned to Christ for spiritual motives, he faced economic disaster.

As I, the missionary, looked at it with the social justice eyes that every missionary has, how could I help these poor peasants who did not pay back what they borrowed? If I paid the money to the money lender and thus redeemed the man and then said to him, "You are not going to have to pay 75% a year anymore. You pay me 6% a year and that will be quite sufficient," he would be overjoyed. But would he pay responsibly what he now owed the mission? That was the key question.

Health Considerations

Oppression in regard to money and the seizure of land was only one of several oppressions. There was also oppression by disease. The healing provided by the mission physician was most welcome. For example, from the village of Dand a prominent and well-landed peasant named Hira Singh came to see me. His first wife was a sister of a prominent man who came to Christ in 1941. Hira Singh had been observing the Christians for a number of years. By his first wife and his second wife he had had six babies. Each had died before it reached the age of three months. His explanation and the explanation of the people in the village was that "evil spirits ate up the children." So when his seventh baby—a boy—was born, he decided to become a Christian and seek the protection of Jesus Christ, the Lord of the spirits, as the Gadarene demoniac found out. He came to the mission hospital when the baby, like all others, became ill. There the child was completely healed. Hira Singh and his nephew and a couple of neighbours became Christian. A small Christian congregation still exists in the village of Dand. Hira Singh in the 1960's built a small church building, paying the entire cost himself.

Police Oppression

Then there was police oppression. About 1900 a group of seven families of inter-related men made an agreement. They came from various villages. They bought land on the edge of the Maniari River and established a new little village called Navalpur. These men had money. They had stolen it.

They were a band of systematic, skillful robbers. While they looked like peasants, acted like peasants, and built houses like peasants, they went out as scouts to villages roundabout to find a house in which lived a well-to-do man, who was reputed to have some hundreds or thousands of rupees in silver or gold. They would observe his goings and comings.

Then on a moonless night the robber team, having walked the intervening 5-15 miles in the dark, arrived at that village at midnight and dug a hole through the foundations and up through the dirt floor. Then they very quietly entered the house, rifled the strong box, and got away without waking anyone. It was a well planned operation, expertly carried out. They developed tools that would dig through a wall quietly. The man who was digging would post scouts on either side. Nobody ever saw him dig. Nobody ever heard him dig. But in the morning the money was gone. The police were greatly troubled by these robberies; but the seven families prospered.

Then the police found traces that led them to search the seven houses in Navalpur. They found some of the stolen property. They didn't have enough evidence to send the men to jail, but they did have enough to put them under surveillance. This meant that at any time, night or day, when the police came, the peasants of Navalpur had to be in that village. They were not permitted to leave the village. Women could go to the bazaar, but the men could not. And certainly at night they were all expected to be in their homes without fail.

This surveillance put an end to the robberies, so the police were certain that they had the right men.

The men under surveillance decided to become Christian. Whether they acted sincerely or insincerely I do not know. It happened in 1916. By the time I got there, 20 years later, these men had grown sons and daughters—all educated in mission schools—and I was personally convinced that they were no longer carrying out robbing expeditions. They had come to the conclusion that robbery did not pay. It was a bad business. They confined themselves to cultivating their eight or ten acres of land.

Nevertheless, the police surveillance continued. Any time, night or day, the police would knock on the door and say, "Where is so-and-so? Get up. Come to the door. Show your face."

Often the police would say, "I need a meal." Sometimes the police would say, "I'm going to spend the night here. I'm going to sleep here." It was charged by the Christians that the police would also say, "I'm going to sleep with your wife, and don't say anything or it will be too bad for you." On occasion the police would say, "I need somebody to carry my box, or my bedding, from here five miles to a village where I have some work. Pick it up and carry it."

The men of Navalpur had to do so without any pay; or else they were reported, harassed, forced to go 20 miles into Bilaspur to answer questions, and the like.

As I observed this surveillance, I became convinced that the police harassment was both unnecessary and unjust. So I went to see the captain of the police. He listened to what I had to say, and then went to get the records. He studied them and then called me. He was direct and very rough. He said, "Look, Mr McGavran, these are dangerous men. Don't interfere with the police."

I replied, "I know these men very well. They were dangerous men but are changed, and your police are needlessly harassing them."

The captain looked me straight in the eye and said, "Keep your hands off. Keep your hands off or I shall report you to the commissioner and your permit to stay in India will be withdrawn."

A few weeks later, by providential circumstances, I caught the police in needless harassment and in making false reports. They reported that on a certain evening at nine o'clock the men weren't there; as a matter of fact I had been in the village, where the men were in a church meeting. When reporting these things to the captain, I said to him, "Captain, I'm for the police. I think they're doing a splendid job, but in this particular case, your men are giving you false reports. Here's one of them."

The end result was that I won for that group of men freedom from the police harassment. It not only helped that group in that particular village, but it helped the Christian cause in other villages. Among the Satnamis I became known as one who would stand up for the rights of people when they were needlessly harassed. Working for social justice is a legitimate Christian activity.

Needless Harassment

One time three men and a woman came to see me. They sat on the verandah of the office while I interviewed people. Finally their turn came. I courteously seated them on a rug. "What's on your mind?" I asked.

Their leader replied, "The police are needlessly harassing me. They are accusing me of robbery. Sahib, I am **not** a robber. So we have decided to become Christians. We came in to seek your protection."

At this the woman broke in and said, "Why don't you tell him the truth? Why do you tell him a lie? He's our friend."

The man looked surprised. I said, "Yes, by all means, tell me the truth. Don't feed me a long story."

The spokesman continued, "What happened was this. We were standing in the village bazaar, buying some glass bangles for my wife. A policeman came up, stood beside her, and began to handle her breasts, and suggest that he would drop by that evening. I gave him a resounding slap so hard that it knocked him to the ground. All this harassment we are suffering has resulted because of that. They are now accusing me of robbing. They are accusing me of being a thief. They are giving me a very bad time. I have to go to Bilaspur several times a month.

I'm losing time. And there is seemingly no end to it. I've decided to become a Christian and seek your protection."

I said, "Very well. I'll look into this case. Where do you live? Who are the respectable men in your village? Who's your malguzar?"

I visited the village and found that the harassed people were respectable peasants. They paid their taxes. They did good work. They were not troublesome. What they had told me was exactly what the malguzar now told me. Everybody knew that it was true. I went to see the magistrate and told him the real situation. I added, "I don't want to put the police in trouble, but that one policeman was doing what you wouldn't want him to do. I thought you might be interested in getting a factual account. I'm sure that it is the truth."

The magistrate looked at me, asked a few questions, and then said, "We'll see what can be done. You may go."

A few weeks later the case was dropped. The man and his wife came to thank me. They asked, "Now when are you going to baptise us?"

I said, "We can't baptise you yet. I don't want to baptise you until you know something about the Christian faith. So we will come to your village and tell you and your comrades about Jesus. We'll stay at a house, not yours, but you arrange for some friend of yours to give us a room in his house or cowshed where we can stay. You two attend all the meetings and work with your friends and fellow Satnamis. During the campaign, we'll hope that a dozen of your families will decide to become Christians."

He replied, "Yes, we are very pleased." He and his wife went out quite happy.

We held the campaign. We had good meetings. He and his wife attended and learned the stories; but they did not lead any other people to accept Christ. Had we baptised the two of them, there would have been one lone family in that far village. So I said to him, "Rather than being baptised now, you two live as unbaptised followers of the Lord. Count yourselves as Christians and get some of your neighbours to gather at your house every evening. Then have one of the boys who is literate read a chapter of the Bible. In the course of the year get other people to attend and see if you can get a group of Satnamis who believe in Jesus Christ as Lord and Saviour. A year from now we'll baptise not just the two of you but a dozen families."

He agreed. But the plan didn't work out. In the course of a year he got cold, and while he was always very friendly when we went there, he decided not to become a Christian. We had helped the man but we did not feel that he had enough conviction, enough belief on the Lord Jesus. If we took in one family only, it would probably not remain Christian. We may have made a mistake. Perhaps we ought to have baptised the couple and thus made them part of the Christian community and trusted that they would win others.

An Axe is Stolen

Another time a man named Akat came to see me. He also reported that the police were harassing him. "Well," I said, "the police are good men. It's a good thing we have police. If we didn't have police, this country would be overrun by thieves and robbers and men who make life miserable. You can thank God there are police."

"Yes," he said, "but they are accusing me of stealing."

"Did you steal?" I asked. "What are they accusing you of stealing?"

"They say I took an axe."

Now an axe is not a big thing; it is worth only 10-15 rupees. I asked, "Did you take it?"

He replied, "I'll tell you the truth. I did take it."

"Where is it?" I asked.

"It is in a neighbouring village."

"Very well, I'll go in with you and speak to the magistrate."

The next time his case came up in court, I went with him. When his name was called, he went in and I went in beside him.

The magistrate looked at me, a foreigner, and asked, "What do you want?"

I replied, "I've come to bear testimony in regard to this man."

He said, "Stand here." He then questioned the man, "What's the charge?"

"Stealing an axe."

"Did you steal it?"

I said, "Akat, tell him the truth."

"Yes, sir, I stole it," Akat affirmed.

The magistrate looked very surprised. "You stole it?" he exclaimed.

Akat responded, "Yes, sir."

I said to the magistrate, "You might ask where it is, sir."

"Where is it, Akat?"

Akat replied, "I hid it in such-and-such a village."

The magistrate asked Akat to step outside. He then spoke to me. "What's happening, Mr McGavran?"

I replied, "This man told me that he was being harassed by the police, and I told him to tell the truth. I came here to see that he did."

The magistrate said, "Very extraordinary. Ordinarily they bring in many witnesses to say they did not do it and the case drags on. I finally come to the conclusion that they did do it and, if the evidence is sufficient, I send them to jail. But this man confesses."

I then told the magistrate that to simplify matters, I had asked Akat two days before to get the axe and give it to me. "It is in my car just outside."

"Go get it," the magistrate said. I did so and laid it on the magistrate's table. He then called Akat and said sternly, "I'm not going to send you to jail this time. I'm going to put you under surveillance for six months. You will report to the police station every week and if we hear any more complaints against you, it will be jail for you. Do you understand?"

Akat said, "Yes, sir, I understand. There'll be no more complaints, sir."

There was a Christian group in Akat's village, and he, his wife, daughter and son started attending the worship services every night. Eight months later he was baptised and remained a good Christian till he died.

Oppression By the Malguzar—Feudal Lord

In that same village in regard to that same man an extraordinary thing happened. After he became a Christian one day he came to Takhatpur in great distress.

"Sir, a terrible thing has happened," he said. "When I and my wife and my son and my daughter were out of the village for a week, the malguzar tore my house down, burned the timbers, broke up the tiles and covered my lot with bricks that the malguzar is assembling to build a house."

"Why did you build a house on land that was not yours?" I asked.

"I didn't, sir. I own the land."

"You do? Quite impossible. A malguzar would never tear down a house on land that you own. How do I know that you own it?"

"Here's the legal deed," he said.

I immediately spread it out and read it carefully. It was written in Hindi. It was a nicely written deed selling this particular piece of property to this particular man for 150 rupees. The man unquestionably owned the land, and this was unquestionably a case of oppression. The malguzar was punishing this man for becoming a Christian. It was a clear case of persecution, so that Satnamis in the surrounding villages would fear to become Christians.

All the Christians in that area were greatly worried. They asked if we could do anything. Finally one of them, who was a rather poor Christian but a very tough man, said, "Why don't we go in there, each one of us carrying some wood, erect a house, build a fire and start cooking a pot of rice? Let Akat and his wife and family all sit in the house cooking their meal. Then the malguzar will not be able to tear it down again. If he does, we'll be there to witness it. Furthermore, since we've built the house, we'll all go to court as witnesses if a case is started."

A week later in a closed session at night a dozen men worked out this plan. All agreed, "We won't do it at night; we'll do it in the day at the crack of dawn. We will throw the bricks off before the malguzar awakes. While half a dozen of us work, the others will be prepared to defend the workers against the malguzar's gangsters whom he will send to beat us up. You, sir, will be a witness to the whole thing."

I pondered that for several days. I didn't tell anybody, because if a story like that gets out, the project cannot be put into operation. I also prayed about it. I finally decided that justice required me to act. We then set a date and assembled the materials that we needed: four corner posts, several intermediate posts, bamboos for the roof and walls and enough grass to make a thatch.

About three in the morning, we set out for the village, each man carrying material for the simple house. By the time the sun was rising, we had cleared the bricks away, dug the holes, and were putting in the posts. At this point the 20-year-old son of the malguzar appeared, very angry. "What are you doing?"

We answered, "This man has a deed to this land signed by your father. We are just building a house for him."

The young man shouted, "You can't do that. If my father were here, he'd have you all beaten up."

"I don't think he would," I said, "because, after all, he is a law-abiding man. His signature is on the deed. He knows the laws of the land. So we're going right ahead."

It was fortunate that the malguzar was away. If he had been there, he would have ordered several of his henchmen to attack us with sticks. There would have been a riot. We probably would have been driven from the place, because his men were expert at stick work. Fortunately, the malguzar was in Bilaspur on a legal case. The young man, his son, however, was intelligent. He sent one of his men running across the fields six miles to the subinspector of police. The subinspector saddled his horse and hurried over. Six miles over, six miles back, about four hours later, up rode the subinspector, very angry. "What are you doing!" he shouted.

While he was supposed to be enforcing the law, actually he was in the pay of the malguzar, who provided all the rice that this subinspector and his family and guests ate every year. Several bags of the best rice in the land went to him each year at harvest time. He was pro-malguzar in any dispute the malguzar had with his tenants.

By the time he arrived, the house had been built, a fire had been kindled, a pot of rice had been put on. The subinspector raged up and down but he could do nothing. He threatened to take me to court. "I shall arrest you for disturbing the peace."

I said, "Go ahead, subinspector. I am a law-abiding man. If you need to arrest me, please arrest me."

He ejaculated, "You will hear from me and from the superintendent of police in Bilaspur."

"You and he both have my address," I said. "I am ready any time."

The day ended with the house standing. Akat and the Christians had won a big victory. All the Christians of the area were feeling very good about the affair. However, that exciting day started for me an eight-month harassment by the police. I had to go several times to Bilaspur. I had often to go to the police station; on numerous occasions they came to see me. Finally, an English officer—it was fortunate this was before 1947 and the district superintendent of police was an Englishman—sent word to the subinspector at Takhatpur, "Settle this case." The subinspector in Takhatpur summoned me and the malguzar and said, "Now look, we need to get this settled. This cannot go on." He asked the malguzar, "What are your conditions?"

The malguzar said, "I'll settle if the missionary will promise never to build a church on that lot. That's what I'm really afraid of. I don't want a church on that corner. That's the most prominent corner in the village. I'm not going to have a church in my village."

The subinspector turned to me. "Do you promise not to build a church there?"

I replied, "Yes. I'm not interested in building a church there. I'm interested in the man getting justice. If the malguzar will give him justice, I'll be pleased to promise that I will never build a church on that land." Thus the matter was settled.

That adventure resounded through the land, and Satnamis everywhere said, "If you really are oppressed, you need to see the McGavran Sahib in Takhatpur." I appeared to them as their champion against injustice. This was not my purpose. I did not know that it was happening; but it unquestionably did happen. McGavran Sahib appeared as a champion of the oppressed.

Malguzars Turn Toward Christ

So much was this the case that one day six men walked in from their village 20 miles away. It was not in the territory where our mission was working, but in that assigned to the Evangelical Mission. These Satnamis were young and middle-aged Satnami malguzars, tall fine-looking men. They came from an aristocratic Satnami family. Amongst the Satnamis there are aristocrats and ordinary people. The aristocrats marry chiefly aristocrats. They tend to be light in colour and tall. They have more land.

The men said, "We are being oppressed by money lenders and Hindu malguzars. Our only hope is to become Christians. So we have come to you."

I responded, "You live south of my territory. I cannot help you; but tell me all about it."

As I listened, I concluded that they were indeed being oppressed. They really wanted as a group to become Christians. To have a group of Satnami malguzars becoming Christians held many possibilities. These men owned more than a hundred acres of land. Their becoming Christian would establish a strong church.

This was happening in the midst of World War II. Petrol was almost unobtainable. I did most of my work on my bicycle. The Manku Ghat Mela, the annual gathering of Christians of Chattisgarh on a 40-acre island for three days of revival meeting, was about to begin. So I said to the six men, "I shall be cycling to Manku Ghat and will stop off at your village and talk with you."

They replied, "Splendid."

On my way home rom the Manku Ghat Mela, I stopped at their village. On the cycle I was carrying a blanket and one half of a small tent. My companion, by name Ishwari Prasad, a pastor-evangelist in a village church, carried the other half of the tent, a blanket, and some cooking utensils.

We set up our tent on the edge of the village, out under a tree, intending to spend the day talking to the Satnami malguzars. However, we found that every man in this village had gone on some enterprise—to collect a debt, settle a marriage case, or attend a wedding. So we talked to the women.

One of them was a Christian from the village of Amora. I said, "I didn't know that you had relatives here."

"Oh, yes," she said, "I belong to the family. That is why they're interested in being Christians. They're responsible people. I hope you take them."

I said, "Gather the women, and I'll tell them about the true religion and the Saviour." We had a good meeting in the morning and another in the afternoon. Then the women dispersed.

One beautiful young woman came up to me and said, "Let me show you around the village. I'm the wife of the leading man. He went up to see you and was very pleased when he came back. I want to show you my house."

Her name was Sahibin. Now "Sahib" means a white man. "Sahibin" means a white woman. The reason she was called Sahibin was because she was very light coloured, and had gray eyes and fine features. When she was born, she was even lighter. As they looked at the baby and admired it, they exclaimed, "Hey, this one looks like a white woman." So they called her "Sahibin." She was open and intelligent. She talked like the mistress of the place. She seated me on her front porch, and we had quite a long talk about Christ, Christianity, the new life and where they would build their church. I was impressed.

Then she said, "Come on inside. Let me show you my house." So I got up and walked through the door into the house where they cooked their food. Suddenly this young woman walked up quite close to me and brushed her breasts across my chest. In the twinkling of an eye, I realised that she was offering herself to me. I felt in the presence of great danger. In less time than it takes to say these words, I turned and headed for the door. As I came out of the door, I saw a 13-year-old girl with her eye glued to a hole in the wall. This was not an accident. This was going to be witnessed. What I did would be well established.

I carried on as if nothing had happened. I sat down again on the porch and said, "You have a large comfortable house." After some further casual conversation, I passed on to other houses in the community and talked to the women there. Ishwari Prasad had been visiting other houses and talking to their occupants.

Toward evening we went out to our tent, cooked the evening meal and prepared to bed-down for the night. After we had eaten and were warming ourselves by the fire, here came Sahibin with a woman companion, one of the older women in the village. Because of the fire there, four of us were clearly visible to everybody in the village. We sat and talked for about an hour about the group's becoming Christian.

What I think had happened was that she had tested me. Perhaps she thought that all men want sexual intercourse and that she would advance the cause of the village by offering herself. When she found that I was living according to Christian principles, she was pleased. It confirmed her belief that the Satnami section of the village, or at least a large part of it, ought to become Christian.

Unfortunately this village was in another mission's territory. I felt myself bound by comity. It would have been difficult for me to baptise people and establish a church in the territory of a sister mission. I did, however, go to the Evangelical Mission station and plead with them to baptise these seekers and see to it that they became good Christians. Unfortunately the mission had no experience of accepting, shepherding and championing such groups. Consequently, it played around with that fine group, but never led it to Christ and never established a church.

Social Justice and Evangelism Summarised

What conclusion can we come to from all these incidents? There were many like them.

First, we must serve the oppressed and battle for justice. We must remove oppression as far as possible.

Second, at the same time we must insist that the removal of oppression and the service of people is not the main purpose of evangelisation. Nor is it the great good of becoming Christian. The great good is receiving eternal life, forgiveness of sins, and God's Word, the Bible, as our Book. The great good is learning what the Bible teaches and living according to it. Not much is gained by a superficial joining of a new human organisation, but much is gained by joining Christ's Body and living as a part of God's Household.

Third, without major turnings to Christ, social improvements of one sort or another are not lasting. They bring little permanent improvement to the whole people. Until multitudes have become Christian and hundreds of churches have been established, a whole caste will not be majorly lifted or improved no matter how much social justice is implemented.

Fourth, in addition to helping remove injustices and oppressions by money lenders, police and others, we must insist on Christians themselves doing right to others. They must learn and obey what the Bible says about righteousness. We must make sure that they regularly and meaningfully worship God. Within their own families they should behave like Christians and in their own village surroundings act honestly and compassionately.

To be sure, they are not responsible for what money lenders or the police do to other people. They have no power over the police or the Hindu money lenders. Consequently, the social justice God wants them to do is what they can do in their own families and their own neighbourhoods. Christians must work for social justice. They can do this in two ways: a) by championing the oppressed; and b) by bringing multitudes of the oppressed to Christ, forming them into permanent Christian congregations, and teaching them to deal justly with others.

"Thus it is written, that the Christ should suffer and on the third day rise from the dead, and that repentance and forgiveness of sins should be preached in his name to all nations, beginning from Jerusalem" (Luke 24:46-47 RSV).

9

Missionary Adventures

Many missionaries meet unusual and dangerous circumstances. There are challenging tasks to do. Their life is not all routine work. It often includes adventure and excitement.

Run Over by an Oxcart

One moonlight night in January 1951, when I was 54 years old, my good friend Paul Tularam, pastor of the village church at Lata, and I planned to cycle out to a new Christian group that had started in a village some three miles north of Takhatpur. The road was a well travelled one. During the rains it became a sea of mud and was impassable, but after the rains ended in October, the ground gradually hardened. After rice harvest in November and early December oxcarts began to roll along this road.

In January the roads were still very rough. Herds of village cattle going out from each village to graze in the uncultivated areas left deep hoof marks that the sun had hardened. The only places where a cycle could be ridden easily were the cart tracks. There the road was smooth. In a few places it was actually dusty. In many more, however, where there had been deep mud, the cart tracks had made channels about six to ten inches deep. The bottoms of these were quite smooth, but occasionally when they got too deep, the cycle pedals would hit the ground as they went round. Then one would have to get off and walk for a while until the ruts got shallower.

The moonlight was bright. Tularam and I were making good progress when suddenly about 50 yards ahead there appeared an oxcart plodding slowly north in the same direction we were going. Its wheels occupied the ruts we were travelling in. So the only thing to do was to get out of the rut and ride our cycles over the bumpy road to the left and right of the cart tracks. It would have been quite useless to shout to the driver to get out of the cart tracks and give us the right of way. Furthermore, it would have taken more time. So Tularam pulled off to the right and I to the left and, pressing heavily on the pedals, made our way over bumps around the cart.

The oxen were plodding along very slowly, less than two miles an hour. When I was about 20 feet ahead of the oxen, I pulled off the rough surface back into the smooth track and with much relief started cycling ahead.

No sooner had I pulled into the track, however, than the driver of the cart, who had been asleep, suddenly woke up. Lashing the oxen vigorously, he urged them forward, and they broke into a gallop. The rut there was six inches deep, and before I could get out of it, the oxen had reached my cycle.

The nose and forehead of the ox on the left side of the cart pushed me off the cycle, and I fell to the ground heavily. The cycle passed under the hooves of this ox and then under the left wheel of the cart.

I was sprawled across the road. My feet were on one side of the left rut, my knees on the other. The eight hooves of the oxen came crashing down around me. Fortunately, none of them was placed on my stomach, my chest, my legs, or my head.

In the twinkling of an eye I was under the cart. I felt the cold of the iron tyre of the left wooden wheel touch my calves, and I jerked my feet toward my head. Otherwise, the left wheel of the cart would have broken both legs.

At the same time the iron axle of the cart encased in a wooden beam six feet long caught me in the middle of the back and pushed me at a rapid pace over the rough middle of the road. I was severely bruised, my clothing was torn, and my skin was cut in a number of places.

Had this continued, I would have suffered very severely. In fact, I probably would have been killed. Fortunately, however, in the providence of God the ruts suddenly grew shallow. The axle lifted and passed over my shoulder. As the oxcart rolled rapidly away, I was left there bleeding, badly bruised, but with no broken bones. Death had been averted. The Lord had truly saved me.

Tularam, who had seen all this from the side of the road, was with me instantly. He asked if I was all right. Gingerly standing up and stamping my feet, I assured him that I was—bleeding in a few places but nothing serious.

"Let us go after that man," he said, "and ask him how he dared attempt a murder on a moonlight night."

So Tularam started running down one side of the rut and I the other.

"How can we stop the cart?" I asked Tularam.

"Very easily," he replied. "I'll go up the right side, and you go up the left. We'll pass the cart and continue until we get to the yoke across the neck of the oxen. Their necks are fastened to the yoke by a rope, a loop of which fits over a pin on the outside of each neck. When I shout, you pull up the pin on your side, and I'll pull up the pin on mine. The oxen's necks will be freed from the yoke, and the tongue of the oxcart will fall to the ground. The oxen will trot on ahead."

It was a simple plan and worked beautifully. A surprised driver was jolted when the tongue of the cart hit the ground. When I tried to talk to him, I found that he was dead drunk. He had no idea of what had happened. After telling him what happened and asking his name and village, we decided to let him go.

We gave up our visit to the Christian group in the nearby village. I was in no condition to lead an evening meeting or even attend one. We walked two miles back to my home. I took a careful bath, put some ointment on my cuts, and went to bed. My friend Tularam also slept at my house that night.

The next day Tularam was quite insistent that we start a law case against the man, whose name and village we had secured. However, it seemed to me that the best thing would be to do nothing. The law case would take a lot of time and money. And while the man would no doubt be punished mildly, it was not worth the effort. Whether that man regaled his grandchildren about how he ran over a white man, I do not know. Probably not. He was too drunk to remember anything. But I thank God for a most remarkable delivery.

Burning Bricks

Like many of my colleagues, I did a good deal of building. In erecting small village churches, the local Christians did most of the work, but the missionary played a part. I also built a hospital. Our supporting church at Fullerton, California, led by Pastor Frank Purnell, lost four young men in World War II. As a memorial it gave $4,000 to build at Takhatpur the Fullerton Temple of Health, the mission hospital. In the closing decades of the 20th century one cannot build much for $4,000; but in 1946 $4,000 enabled me to erect a small but adequate hospital. Of course, I watched every penny and made the money go as far as possible.

For example, I could have bought bricks at, let us say, 200 rupees a thousand. But I could have bricks made and burned for 100 rupees a thousand, and thus save a great deal of money. I hired villagers who dug the clay, added water, trampled it into smooth mud, slapped it into moulds and set row after row of wet bricks in the sun to dry.

The $4,000 had arrived in October. I already had bought an acre of land on the edge of the town. In early January I had drafted the plans for the hospital, and after making some improvements, the Mission Medical Committee had passed them and authorised construction.

In February, knowing that wood or coal would be needed to burn the bricks, I heard that powdered coal, called slack, was available very cheap from a mine about 200 miles away. I bought 20 tons. It would be sent down by rail to arrive in April.

I then hired villagers to make 100,000 sun-dried bricks. They dug the clay, carried the water, trampled the wet lumps into smooth mud, slapped it into moulds, turned them over, and there gleaming in the sun were wet soft bricks. These in three days would be bone dry, hard and ready to be stacked in a kiln for burning in early May.

Making a kiln is an interesting process. The men who make the bricks spread a layer of wood or coal and a layer of bricks on top of that. Then they spread another layer of wood and another layer of sun-dried bricks and so on until the kiln is complete, a mound 20 feet in diameter and 10 feet high. Then they plaster the whole thing over with mud. At the height of the hot season, May, they light the bottom. In two weeks they take out burned bricks.

Since April 30th passed and my 20 tons of coal had not arrived, I hastily bought wood and burned the 100,000 bricks in the middle of May. I did not dare wait. The rainy season was fast approaching, and sun-dried bricks melt in the rains.

In early June, just before the rains, a fellow missionary wrote me saying, "McGavran, there are five railway wagons down here with coal in them. Your name is on them. And they are accumulating demurrage in the railway yards."

I dropped all my other work and hurried in to the Bilaspur railway station, 23 miles, by cycle. The five wagons were accumulating demurrage and the powdered coal in those wagons in the fierce heat of May had begun to combust spontaneously. In each of the wagons it was beginning to burn! The wagons would have been burnt up if the coal had remained in them. In great haste I hired coolies and had all the coal shovelled out into 15 piles beside the tracks. From three of them little columns of smoke were coming up. Despite the shovelling, the slack coal was still burning there on the ground.

I paid the demurrage and the coolies and hurried off to town to hire 20 carts. I then hired some more coolies to pour water on the coal, put out the fires, and shovel it into the carts which that night set off for Takhatpur, 23 miles away. It was an all-night trip by oxcart. I cycled home by moonlight arriving at ten o'clock.

Before going to bed I had to decide where to put the powdery hot coal. I couldn't use it! It was the beginning of the rains, but it would lie there, I thought, until next year. However, seeing those columns of smoke rising from the piles of coal beside the railway tracks made me anxious. If powdered coal is stacked anywhere, it's likely to combust spontaneously. If I put the slack inside any room and it begins to burn, it will burn the roof off and destroy the building.

Knowing something about the laws of burning, I resolved to stack it in a room and plaster the room shut—plaster the door shut, plaster the windows shut, and put a six-inch cover of mud over the top of the pile! Thus not a breath of air could get in. Then I was confident that the coal, lacking oxygen, would not burn.

There was a spare room in a nearby building the mission owned. Into that 12 x 12 room the coal was poured. It filled the room to a height of about eight feet. The workmen plastered the door and windows shut and put a cap of mud over the whole. There it was safe and sound for the next ten months. In April of the next year we would take it out and burn more bricks.

Along in August, however, the caretaker of the hospital came to see me early one morning. "Sir, the walls of that room where you stored the coal. . . . The walls are getting very hot. Furthermore, there is a column of smoke coming out through the roof."

I jumped on my bicycle and raced down to the hospital, about a half a mile. Sure enough, that was exactly what was happening. I put my hand on the wall and almost burned it. The whole wall was hot! I wondered how in the world this could have happened. Where was the fire getting the air? As I walked around the room, what had happened became clear. The weight of the coal had spread the wall, and in the back there was a crack a couple of inches wide through which air was streaming into the pile of powdered coal. A brisk fire was burning.

Fortunately that spring, as part of building the hospital, I had decided to dig a well and had gone down ten feet, but had not struck any sign of water. At the same time another exploratory well had struck water at ten feet, so we had abandoned the first hole. The circular hole was ten feet deep, eight feet wide, and full of rain water!

Here was the perfect solution. We threw the coal into that hole full of water. It could never catch fire. No oxidisation could take place. In May of the next year the coal would be in as good shape as the day we put it in.

The next year, a local contractor came and said to me, "I want to buy that coal and make the bricks you need for further building."

I asked, "Will you pay the right price for the coal and sell me the bricks at the right price?"

He answered, "I'll pay whatever you say and sell you the bricks cheaper than you can make them."

We drew up and signed a contract and in June he delivered another 100,000 bricks.

Yes, there are adventures in the missionary's life!

Getting Stuck in the Mud

While I was living in Fosterpur, one of the Christians living in a village two miles away was on his roof in the rain repairing it. His foot slipped, he rolled off the roof and cracked a collar bone and a rib. He soon developed a high fever. His fellow Christians carried him about eight at night to Fosterpur. I was afraid he had some internal injuries. He must be taken ten miles to the Mungeli hospital at once. He might be dead by morning. I would take him in the car. This was in 1938, before the war, so we had plenty of petrol.

We started out about 8:30. It was dark and rainy. Half way to Mungeli there was a very muddy stretch where a trickle of water flowed across the road. The ruts were very deep and full of water. The sick man was in the back seat with his wife, groaning and complaining. I put the car into low gear and tried to move through the deep mud. Soon the car ground to a halt. The wheels whirred. We had no traction.

I then remembered that about 200 yards off the road there was a village. As I looked in that direction I thought I saw a faint glow. Possibly that was the village. I started out in the dead dark, splashing my way across rice fields, water up to my knees. Every now and then I came to a dike, a *bund* they called it, made of earth, between two fields. I clambered up this side, slid down the other and splashed my way across another field, hoping that I would not tread on a cobra or other poisonous snake.

Finally I came to the village and received a surprisingly cordial welcome. When I told them the problem, the young men of the village exclaimed, "Of course we'll help you! Come along!"

They brought a lantern and we started back along a good path, somewhat slippery with the rain, but otherwise good. We were soon back to the car. Eight men on one side, and eight on the other. I was at the wheel. I started the engine and they pushed. Before you could say Jack Robinson, the car was through the long muddy stretch.

I said to the villagers, "Thank you very much. How much do I owe you?"

They replied, "Sahib, it was nothing. We're glad to do this. Anytime you get in trouble, let us know. If you're taking a villager in because he's broken a rib and is about to die, we can't do less than push your car."

I thanked them cordially, bade them good bye and in a short time arrived at the mission hospital. My village friend received instant treatment. By morning his fever was down and he was out of danger.

Rafting Does Not Work

Adventures like the above are a common part of the life of a missionary; but the next adventure I relate was a bit unusual. In building the hospital, I had observed that the way to get wood for the rafters, beams, door and window frames was to buy sal logs. Sal is a durable wood. Termites will not eat it. Sal trees grow in the big forest, about 25 miles north of Takhatpur, across the fertile plain. Villagers go up and buy sal trees from the government officer, the ranger, who manages the forest. They fell these, trim off all the branches and load the logs onto carts. Then a pair of oxen, or more likely a pair of buffalos, which are stronger than oxen, pulls each cart to Takhatpur. By that time the logs are fairly expensive.

I remembered the river that flows out of that forest right past Takhatpur. We could buy the trees in the jungle, fell them, and push them into the dry river bed. We would tie them together into a raft and wait for the big flood to float them down to Takhatpur. We could get the logs quite cheaply, paying only the cost of felling them, trimming them, and pushing them into the dry river bed. Being a prudent man, however, I thought it wise to make a trial run with one small raft.

In January I went up to the jungle and bought five trees. A forest inspector walked through a patch of forest on the edge of the river and told us which sal trees we could cut. We felled five trees, cut each in two, pushed the ten logs into the river bed and made a raft. There it stood on dry ground. When in July a huge rain would come and this river flowed ten feet deep, we would float them down. Quite pleased with myself, I went back to Takhatpur.

That rainy season (June through September) I waited until the river had filled up and there was assurance of a big rain coming. Then I drove in my car to within two miles of the raft and turned the car over to the driver to take back to Takhatpur. An Indian helper and I got on the raft, which was floating at the end of a rope, and cut it loose from the bank. We started moving quietly down the river—a very pleasant journey! The river carried us along with no effort at all. Occasionally there would be a tree hanging over the river. Several times we almost got brushed off by low-hanging branches.

Then the excitement began. As we sailed across a bar on which grew several trees, the ropes on the bottom of the raft caught on a root in the bottom of the river. The raft on which we were sitting suddenly stood upright and would have fallen on top of us, except that I jumped out one way and my helper jumped out the other. In falling, the raft loosened itself from the root and started floating off down the river. We swam after it, climbed on board, and continued our pleasant quiet journey. A couple of deer came down to drink. Goats and cattle grazed along the banks. Birds were abundant. It was a lovely journey.

About three that afternoon we were passing a big village, and the river was wide and very shallow. A young woman was filling her water pot. She called out and asked, "Where are you going?"

I said, "We're going to Takhatpur. Would you like to come along?"

That was exactly the wrong thing to say. She thought I was making an immoral suggestion. She lit in and subjected me to five minutes of the most vigourous, colourful, abusive language I have ever heard. My Indian companion (my employee, by the way) was listening with a good deal of amusement, as his sahib was getting a thorough dressing down. At just that time, the raft grounded on a shallow sandy place in the river. There we were stuck, listening to this young woman's vile tongue lashing. We got off the raft, dug it free, pushed out into deeper water, and somewhat red-faced, continued on down the river.

That night about 6:30, we were passing another village and a man on the bank called out, "You'd better be very careful. Right around that turn there's a big waterfall. If you go over that, you'll be killed!"

I said to my companion, "I didn't know there were any waterfalls in this river. Let's spend the night in this village. We'll look at the waterfall in the morning."

We pulled the raft up on the shore as far as we could. It was very heavy, and we couldn't get it up more than a couple of feet. We tied it to a big rock and went up into the village. We inquired and found that the schoolhouse was empty, and asked if we could spend the night in it. They said yes. The schoolmaster very kindly sent in a meal of rice and cooked vegetables. I had a mosquito net, which I wore during the day as a turban. I tied the net to a couple of chairs, crawled into it and lay down on the bare floor, safe from the mosquitoes buzzing around. Soon we were both asleep.

In the middle of the night a torrential rain came on. It thundered on the roof. Buckets of water came down! As I listened to it for ten minutes, fifteen minutes, a half an hour, I said to myself, "The river will be rising, and our raft will just float away. Then here we will be, stuck many miles from Takhatpur."

I woke my companion, who was sleeping through the downpour. We felt our way in the pouring rain, through ankle-deep mud down the village street. It was as slippery as slippery could be, down the bank of the river. Our raft was indeed about to break loose. It was bobbing around in the water, held by the rope that was slipping off that rock. We pulled it up another few feet, tied it more securely to the rock, sloshed our way back and slept the rest of the night.

In the morning we walked down stream to look at the waterfall. It was truly a waterfall. The water fell for about ten feet and then went cascading down a rapids for 150 yards. Beyond, the river flowed quietly again. We tied the raft to the bank 50 yards above the falls. Then I walked downstream to the big pool where the rapids ended, and I waited. My helper loosed the logs one by one and let the river carry them to me. As each log came down, I dove in and brought it to shore and tied it fast. In three hours we had all the logs down and a new raft made. We floated along merrily.

For about ten miles we floated on quietly, a very pleasant journey. No rush, no push, the raft made good time without any labour. We had nothing to do. We listened to the birds sing, watched the cattle graze and saw the fish jump out of the water. We were having quite a lark.

Then suddenly we heard another waterfall. The river began to hasten. Realising the danger, we made for the bank and tied the raft fast to a big tree. I said to my helper, "Repeat the process. I'll go below the falls. You loose the logs one by one."

I waited at the pool below the falls, but no logs came. An hour and a half, and not a log! My helper then appeared. He had loosed the logs all right, but the current had carried them out to the middle of the river and lodged them on an island. All the logs were out where we couldn't get to them and send them on their way. That ended the adventure.

We walked on a few miles to a small town called Lormi and bought a couple of pounds of *jalebis*. We had had nothing to eat all day and were hungry. We then walked on about six miles through pouring rain, crossing two small streams, flowing chest deep across the road, and came to the house of a village Christian friend. He took us in and fed us. I went to bed with a fever. But by morning the fever had gone, and we walked on our way 12 miles into Takhatpur. We had learned that the best and cheapest way to get logs down was the way the villagers had been doing it for hundreds of years!!

Compromise—A Christian Necessity

We had a number of adventures over the boundaries of land. For example, I had purchased an acre of low-lying land right in the middle of Takhatpur and across a little stream that flowed in the rains and was dry the rest of the year. When the deputy commissioner, who was the highest officer in the district, visited Takhatpur he said, "I want to see the site of this hospital you are going to build."

I took him to the site. He exclaimed, "You're not going to put the hospital on this low-lying land that might be flooded. Why don't you get that high land east of it?"

I replied, "I would be very pleased to get those fields but the six owners won't sell them to me."

He turned to the *patwari* and said, "Call in the six owners of these pieces of land."

The *patwari* rushed off and in half an hour had all six of them standing there. The deputy commissioner, Rai Bahadur Sanyal, a Hindu gentleman, said to them, "Look, this missionary wants to build a hospital here. It will be for the good of the town. You'll have medical services such as you would not otherwise have. I understand that you won't sell your six small pieces of land to him. You ought to be very pleased to do so."

He waited a minute, but nobody spoke up to say, "Yes, sir, we are very pleased to sell it." So Mr Sanyal then said, "This is a public project. The government is indebted to the mission for putting in this hospital. If you won't sell the land to him willingly, I will have to acquire it through government processes."

There was again dead silence. "And," he went on, "if the government acquires the land, it will pay you a minimum price, whereas if you sell it to the missionary, he will pay a fair market price for it. Now do you have anything to say?"

All six immediately replied, "Sir, we'd be very pleased to sell our land to him and honoured to have the hospital built on land that was formerly ours."

The deputy commissioner turned to me, "Take these men into the headquarters town, Bilaspur (22 miles distant), and have them execute sale deeds. And give them a good price for it too." Then he said to the *patwari*, the local land record officer in Takhatpur, "Go with them and see that everything is done properly." Then turning to me he said, "Dr McGavran, you now have enough land to put a very good hospital here. I hope that you do so."

Thus was the land purchased. We built the hospital and all the quarters that were needed. We cultivated part of the higher ground, and the income was used to support the hospital.

One day I said to Dr C B Lal, "We really ought to have a fence along that side of the property, because the village cattle come in and graze round the buildings and stand on the porch of the hospital and leave deposits."

He replied, "Yes, I thoroughly agree."

I called the *patwari* and said, "Please measure with your chain officially so that there will be no mistakes and tell us where our boundary lies. I'll have a fence put on the property line you determine."

He took a half a day measuring it from one official boundary pillar and then another. We drove in pegs as he would say, "This is the boundary line."

The boundary ran up, not where we had supposed, but over the bank of a *talao*, that is, a small artificial pond about 100 by 100 feet in dimension, which one of the prominent malguzars had had built there as an act of merit to serve the people of the town. We put our fence exactly where the *patwari* had told us the boundary lay. The corner post was driven into the water about three feet from the edge. This seemed to us to be a good arrangement. We now had access to water the year round.

The next day the malguzar heard that we had claimed a portion of his land on which he had built a public pond. He stormed down furiously with ten men, tore up the fence and re-erected it on our land 25 feet from the line the *patwari* had set. We were losing a strip of land 25 feet wide and perhaps 200 feet long. Dr Lal came to me in considerable agitation, "What should we do?"

I replied, "Let's call the *patwari* and find out where the line actually lies. Perhaps he made a mistake."

The *patwari* declared, "I measured it yesterday."

I replied, "Please measure it again today, just so there can be no mistake." He measured it and the line lay beyond question where we had put up the fence. By law we had a portion of the *talao*!! The malguzar was present on the second day.

I said to him, "You see what the *patwari* says. But I quite grant your point that the land that slopes down toward the water is properly a part of your *talao*. The trouble has arisen because you built one side of your *talao* on the land of another man. But all that is past history. I'll put our fence now at the top of your bank, somewhat down toward our property so that a person can walk around the *talao* on the top of the bank and never be on our property at all. Does this suit you?"

The malguzar was surprised and pleased. He had not been accustomed to any such friendly adjudication of disputes. He had anticipated a law suit. He became our fast friend.

Cultural Adjustments in Marriage

Perhaps the most interesting adventures lay in the field of marriage adjustments. While the law in India after the 1930's required that marriages be made after the age of twelve or fifteen, child marriage continued to be practiced amongst most of the residents of Chattisgarh, and most of the castes celebrated the permanent marriage ceremony at a very early age. Two families living in separate villages decided that an infant boy in one village would be married to an infant girl in another. The boy's parents paid a substantial sum of money to the girl's parents. The ceremony was performed. The girl stayed in her parents' home awaiting puberty.

Then within six months or a year after the girl had her first menstrual period a "going-away" ceremony was performed. She then went to her young husband's home in a distant village and lived there as a married woman. Since she went there as a girl of twelve or thirteen, she sometimes found a mother-in-law or a husband or circumstances that she could not tolerate. So after a few months or a year she ran back to her own home and declared emphatically that she would never live with her husband. She then became a young woman looking for a new husband.

Anyone who took her as his wife would have to pay the first husband a considerable sum of money. A band of eight to twenty men from the first husband's village would go to the village of the young man with whom she now lived and demand payment of money. Since all concerned agreed that this was the just and lawful thing to do but also a grievous burden, settling the amount of money and securing payment generally caused a considerable hassle. Sometimes the group of men from the first husband's village would have to make two or three journeys to the new village before they secured the right number of rupees.

In one of the villages where a group of Satnami families had become Christian, a couple of years after their baptism the daughter of one of these families, married three years before into a distant village, decided she could no longer tolerate her husband's home and ran back to her parents. Since she now lived with Christians and—horror of horrors—ate with Christians, her husband could no longer take her back. Until she got married again—i.e., went to live with some other man—her husband could claim no repayment of the bride price his parents had paid when he was a boy of three.

A year after this young woman returned to her mother's house, ate with Christians, worshiped with them, she was baptised. Soon after that her father and the father of a Christian young man in a village six miles away decided that she would become the wife of this Christian young man. He had just returned from boarding school.

Shortly after this second marriage a group of men from her first husband's village, each armed with a *lathi*, a six-foot-long solid bamboo stick, appeared at her new husband's village. In God's providence I was preaching in that village that night and was present when the first husband's party of debt collectors arrived.

After considerable conversation between the two groups, to which I listened with interest, the Christian group asked me, "Would you sit down with us and become part of the deciding group?"

So I and four Christians sat down with five non-Christians from the first husband's village. They poured out in the centre of that circle of ten men about 50 small white snail shells. Cowries, they were called. The ten men seated themselves so that a man representing the new husband sat next to one representing the former husband. The man to my left started the process.

Each cowrie shell represented ten rupees. The first man representing the Hindu husband picked up 20 shells, 200 rupees. He picked up another one and then threw it back. Two hundred rupees was all that he thought his party ought to ask. He then passed the 20 shells to his left, a Christian who represented the new husband. This man, who utterly rejected the idea that the new husband, his cousin, would pay 200 rupees, threw back 14 cowrie shells one by one. He was saying in effect, "Sixty rupees is all this man is going to pay." He then passed the shells to the next man, who added 20 shells. He was saying in effect, "This young man has to pay 260 rupees."

So the shells passed to each of the ten men. The first time around all the men representing the first husband were demanding 200 or more rupees, and the men representing the second husband declared they were going to pay 60 or 70 rupees.

Then the cowrie shells went around the group a second time. This time the representatives of the first husband, evidently seeing that no solution was possible on these terms, came down from 20 cowrie shells (200 rupees) to 12 (120 rupees). When the 12 cowrie shells were passed to me, I decided to up what had to be paid to 80 rupees, so I took the 12 cowrie shells handed to me by the man on my right, threw back 4 and passed 8 to the next man.

After the shells went around the circle the fifth time, everybody was agreed that 8 cowrie shells was about the right price—80 rupees. The family of the Christian young man, the second husband, paid 80 rupees to the ten men armed with *lathis* and the case was amicably settled. The missionary concerned—myself—also had received a firstclass lesson in cultural adjustment.

The second adventure in cultural adjustments in marriage took place when I visited a small Christian community in a section of the Bilaspur District that was managed by another missionary. The fifteen-year-old daughter of one of the Christians whose first marriage—like most—had not worked out was living at home. Suddenly without consulting her family she ran away with a young man visiting in the neighborhood and went to a distant village in my part of the district. Her father said to me, "If you will take me in your car to that village in the morning, we will arrive when the men of the village are all out working in the fields. My daughter will be alone in the house. I will go in and seize her, carry her to the car, push her in, and we will bring her home."

I debated the matter with him somewhat, but since he was quite sure that the girl's decision had been a mistaken one, I agreed to his proposal.

When we got to the distant village, we stopped outside the man's house. The father rushed in, grabbed the girl, brought her out, and pushed her into the car. He slammed the door, and I reached for the key to start the car.

Unfortunately, at just that moment the young husband came up, reached in through the front window, seized the car key, pulled it out of its slot, and stood there with the key in his hand. The father, the girl, and I were in the car immobilized in a hostile village.

A crowd was gathering. It was a dangerous situation. It was impossible to move. The crowd could very well maintain that the father had broken into somebody's house and had committed a crime. So I said to the young man, "We will put out the girl on the right side of the car, and as we open the door for her, you give me the key. We will then go on, and the girl will remain with you."

Fortunately he agreed. The girl was put out. The key was handed to me, and we left the village as rapidly as possible. Had we remained there another minute, there would certainly have been a riot, and the father and I would have been beaten. I resolved never again to engage in this kind of a rescue mission. This part of the old culture was something with which I would have no dealings.

A Hospital Seen as Essential

A small early adventure had momentous effects. During the rainy season of 1941, when I was new to the area, I walked in from a long tour in the villages late one night. I had left a distant village about sunset when the moon was shining brightly. Before I had gone five miles, the wind blew up and clouds covered the moon. It became pitch dark and started to rain. I found myself proceeding in dead darkness, hoping that I would stay on the road. As long as I felt mud under my feet, I knew I was on the road. When I began to get thorns in my right hand or my left, I knew I was off the road and was brushing the thorn fence. I proceeded on very slowly, came to the river, crossed it about breast deep, and walked through the town toward my bungalow, which lay on the far side of the town. I expected to get home about twelve o'clock.

When I was going through the town, I thought I'd better stop in and look at the little room in which Dr Philip James occasionally kept inpatients. That was before the hospital was built. There was no hospital at all in Takhatpur. The mission rented two little rooms off the main street of Takhatpur as a dispensary. Dr James each day sat in the front room, right on the street. In the spare room back of that now and then he kept patients who had to stay overnight. If I had not been passing this at midnight, the incident I relate would never have occurred. I would never have gone down there unless Dr James had taken me. But since I was passing it, and since I had the key to the dispensary in my pocket together with all the other necessary keys that a missionary carries around with him, I thought I would just step in and see what it looked like at midnight. I opened the door, went into the dispensary and lit the lantern.

Everything was quiet. The tables and chairs were in proper order.

I opened the door to the inner room and there lying on the floor was a thirty-year-old women completely naked. She had gone to bed on an examining table about three feet high and had either slipped off or had gotten off and lain down on the floor, leaving her sari, which she had spread out under her, on the examining table. She was sound asleep. The lantern cast an eerie light over the small room. I saw a large scorpion crawling across the floor in search of prey and stepped on it. The woman didn't wake. I debated whether to wake her up, which would be very embarrassing for her, or just what to do. Since the night was getting a bit cool, I picked up the sari that she had folded and put on the examining table, covered her quietly, went out, closed the door, locked the front door and went on home.

This incident underlined for me the desperate need in our area for a proper hospital. To run a dispensary was good, but it was not enough. To put such patients as had to stay overnight in a bare inner room where scorpions scuttled across the floor at night was not good. The doctor lived a half mile away and would never come to the dispensary in the middle of the night. The patient might very well die in the night or some unfortunate occurrence take place. Such an arrangement was not good enough for a Christian hospital.

The next day as I was talking this over with Dr James, I said, "We must get a piece of land, and we must build at least the beginnings of a hospital." The story I told about the purchase of the acre of low-lying land and the way in which Mr Sanyal, the deputy commissioner, helped us get some further land all came as a result of this.

Aid From an American Army Chaplain

Another step in the building of a hospital was one of those strange events that convinced me that God looks after His own. All this was happening in the midst of World War II. In December 1941, because of Pearl Harbor, America had leaped into the war and by 1943 was sending her soldiers by way of Bombay across India and then flying them over the Hump in north Burma into China to help Chiang Kai-shek in his tremendous campaign against the Japanese, who had conquered most of China. Since it was much cheaper, quicker and easier to fly the American troops, munitions, food and medicine over the eastern edge of the Himalayas than to walk them over, the army plan was to establish a large military air base in the eastern end of Assam. From there troop-carrier planes flew troops, ammunition and needed supplies into China over the Himalayas. The operation was a large one. Eighty planes a day flew over the Hump. In the course of the next two years 2,000 planes crashed in the eastern Himalayas.

One of the troop-carrier outfits had a chaplain who was a friend of mine. He had been corresponding with me through the years. When he found he was only 700 miles by railway from where I lived, he decided to use his vacation to come over and see me. He wrote telling me that he was coming. I made arrangements to meet him at the rail head (Bilaspur), brought him by car to Takhatpur, walked him around the villages, showed him the desperate need for a hospital. I told him about the little dispensary and the room where I had found the woman, and in short shared the opportunities and problems with him.

I told him that the middle of the rains, when he came, was not a very good time to hunt tigers in the big jungle 20 miles north of us. If he wanted to, however, we'd take a couple of cycles and go up as far as we could and see what we could get.

We got a hunting permit and spent three or four days in the government jungle. We didn't get any game but we had an exciting time. He never forgot that 25-mile walk and a hunt in the big jungle. We did come across a tiger kill—where a tiger had killed an elk four or five days previously. There were the bones and the antlers. Since the tiger might come back to the kill for the last time that night, we built a small *machan* (platform) in a tree 20 feet from the kill and sat up there that night waiting for the tiger to come. But alas, the tiger never came back to the bones and the antlers.

The chaplain, back at his post, wrote me saying,

> I talked to the other Christians in this outfit, and we've agreed to send you our offerings month by month to build one of the wards that you so desperately need. We don't want naked women lying on the floor in our mission hospital!

I wrote him immediately that we'd be very pleased to get the money, that it was an act of God. We'd call this ward the Troop-Carrier Ward. True to his word, he sent money as long as the troop-carrier outfit was in India. When it flew over the Hump into China, he continued sending the monthly offerings. They amounted to $2,000 and enabled us to put up a good ward at the hospital. It was our first building.

It is in this way that any mission project prospers. A plan to get money in this fashion, a plan to build a troop-carrier ward could not have been conceived. But we serve God who does the impossible. And when events of this sort happen, we use them to His glory.

Missions Carry on a Vast Educational Enterprise

Any new Christian community in any part of the world brings many new responsibilities. Christians from amongst the oppressed and the poor of the world, the poverty-stricken thousands come to Christian faith as illiterates. They are not able to read and they have no desire to learn to read. They think all that is beyond them. So classes in literacy must be held in connection with brief nightly worship services.

Furthermore, such communities have large numbers of young people in them, boys and girls at an impressionable age, highly teachable, able to learn. Unfortunately, in the 1940's the pre-Christian communities made no provision for their youth to learn anything other than the traditional way of life. Consequently, for me the establishment of village schools seemed desirable. Christian truth needed to be learned.

Until Christians learn the Apostles Creed, the Ten Commandments, the Lord's Prayer, and the 23rd Psalm, until they know and can tell the essential stories of the life of Jesus Christ our Lord (His birth, wonderful works, sacrificial death and resurrection), they have very little reason to live as Christians or commend the faith to others. So Christian schools in which such essential knowledge can be systematically taught to the oncoming generation are a necessity.

As a result, the missionary enterprise around the world has been in the past and is today a tremendous educational enterprise. In the 1940's more than half of all missionaries who went abroad from North America and Europe went as educational missionaries. They got into school work. Missionary ladies ran girls boarding schools and girls day schools. Men ran boys schools and co-educational schools, primary schools, middle schools, high schools, colleges and seminaries. The missionary enterprise has been a vast educational undertaking.

Our work at Takhatpur was no exception. In the years 1940-42 as we started to get small village churches here and there and the Christian community increased by 100, 150, or 200 souls per year, it became obvious that if we were going to hold these people, if they were going to become good Christians, their boys and girls would have to be educated. This could not happen while they were living in the village, where there were at that time no schools. It could happen only if their mothers and fathers would send them off to boarding school.

A Boarding School is Born

Our mission had a boys boarding school and a girls boarding school, but at a very long distance from Takhatpur. The village parents were unwilling to send their sons and daughters away a couple hundred miles to a mission boarding school. It became clear to me, therefore, that we would have to establish a boarding school for boys primary classes and middle classes. Eventually some of the best would attend high school classes. There were a few primary schools out in the villages, so we encouraged parents to send to them their little children (boys seven, eight, nine, ten and eleven). A few villages were so far from any schools at all that the only way for boys living in them to get an education was to come at the tender age of seven or eight and become boarders in a Takhatpur school.

When I put this need up to the mission—my missionary colleagues—they quite understandably said, "Look, we have a boarding school system established. Building a new institution, staffing it and getting government grant is rather a big proposition, and frankly looks competitive to us. If your village boys won't go to the existing boarding school, 200 miles away, they'll simply have to remain without education."

I tried to get action from the mission convention and the mission executive committee but failed. They took a firm position that they were not going to start a new boarding school at Takhatpur.

We solved the problem in the following way. At Takhatpur, some 20-25 years before, one of the missionaries, Charles Benlehr, had established a small leprosy home. He had secured a lease of some ten acres of land from the government and on it had built housing for 50 lepers, store rooms for food for the year, rice and other grains, a chapel, a row of houses for the leprosy home staff and a small dispensary. Some 25 miles away there was a big leprosy home run by the Evangelical Synod. A hundred miles away was another fine leprosy home managed by the General Conference Mennonite Mission.

It seemed to me that we would be far better advised to use our leprosy facilities for a boys boarding school than to use them to look after men and women afflicted with leprosy, practically none of whom were local people. These poor souls had been gathered up in desperate condition from various parts of the country and were complete strangers in our locality. None had homes. None had been born within 50 miles of our leprosy home.

When I found that the Evangelical and Reformed and the Mennonite Missions would gladly accept about 25 leprosy patients each, I said to our mission, "Here we have a plant that will cost us nothing. There will have to be some repair. We shall have to make sure the buildings are thoroughly sterilised. The buildings are on a beautiful site beside a small river, called the Rahan. Rather than maintain the leprosy home, we should, for the spread of the Christian faith, turn this into a boys boarding school."

The mission listened to my plea and urged that I get a grant from the government to run a middle school. All the signs seemed to be go.

In February 1944, we took 25 leprosy patients by night to the leprosy home at Champa and two nights later repeated the night journey to the Baitalpur home with 25 patients.

We took the tiles off the roof of all buildings occupied by the lepers, so that the sun could stream in and sterilise the walls. We dug a foot of dirt off the floors and brought in new dirt from across the river on which lepers had not walked, so that all these houses where the boys would stay would be fresh and clean. After the blazing sun of March, April and May had shined on the walls for three months, we put the roofs back on, whitewashed the walls, painted the wood posts that held up the verandah roof, and were ready to admit the boys on the 1st of July.

That first year 50 boys came. The school prospered. The boys' parents paid small fees for their instruction. Many Hindu boys from the surrounding villages who had been anxious to go on to school but had no place to go walked in two, three, four or even five miles daily. They paid fees. We got government grants to run a vernacular middle school. Grants for an Anglo-vernacular middle school would be obtained three years later.

Five years later when the school was thriving, we decided to expand it into a high school. There had been a steady demand for this. The Hindu and Satnami boys from the surrounding ten miles were very anxious for us to establish such a school. Bit by bit with money which had been sent me by friends in America, I purchased small pieces of land along the south side of the Rahan River, just opposite the former leprosy home. This was a very good buy, because this was hard sandy soil, whereas most of the soil in that area was heavy black clay. We called it black cotton soil. Any structure built on black cotton soil cracked, but if built on hard sandy soil, it stood like a rock. I was very pleased to get this desirable land, a long narrow strip 60 yards wide and 200 yards long, on which the school, a missionary's residence and some residences for staff were constructed.

The money for all this building came as a gift from Brother Brooks, a Christian businessman in North Carolina who wanted to give $10,000 to the Lord's work. We were pleased to get it, and by being exceedingly economical in our plans and our building, by burning all our own bricks and buying our wood carefully, we managed to erect an adequate high school.

One of our missionaries, Mrs Mary Pollard, had come out as a single missionary with the McGavrans in 1923. She married a British official in 1932. In 1951, when her husband died, she came back to India and became the principal of the Brooks High School near Takhatpur. Thus, bit by bit, the Lord solves problems, opens doors and prospers the work.

A City of Refuge is Founded

In 1943 the Japanese had conquered Siam, now called Thailand, had conquered Burma, were marching across the eastern edge of India, had dropped a few bombs on Calcutta and on the eastern coast of India just 300 miles southeast of Takhatpur. It looked to the allied forces as if Japan would invade India. Consequently, they decided to send a considerable army to meet them. The place they chose to establish the base for this army was the Bilaspur District, where we were working.

One day in May an officer came and said, "We have decided to make an artillery range of the land lying immediately south and east of Takhatpur, seven miles long, seven miles wide."

"You can't do that.!" I ejaculated. "This is full of people."

He said, "Mr McGavran, this is war. The people will have to get out." That was the government order and they announced, "Three weeks from now everybody must be out of this 49-square-mile tract."

It was disastrous for the thousands who lived in that large area, but that was the order. That the military added, "After the war your land will be returned to you and you will be fully recompensed" was not comforting in May 1943.

Some of the Christians lived in villages in that section of the land and had to move. I have already recounted that, had we been able to help the non-Christian relatives of the Christians, this occasion might have led to a great ingathering. But since our funds were severely limited, we could help only the Christians.

All this was happening at the end of the great depression and the middle of World War II. The funds the missionary society had sent to India in 1932 had been halved, and we were carrying on mission with very scanty financing.

Under these circumstances the fortuitous purchase of six acres of good land on the edge of Takhatpur proved providential. In 1941-42, sensing the Christian community would likely increase, and being confident that as it did, more and more of them would come to Takhatpur, the market center, and settle there, I had purchased about six acres of good sandy soil. This was about a quarter of a mile from the mission bungalow and a quarter of a mile from the hospital.

In May 1943 it was lying there unused. So I said to the Christian refugees who had been driven off their land, "We'll buy a thousand rupees worth of bamboos and give each of you enough to build a good shelter. You make this your home."

We called it Sharan Nagar, the City of Refuge. On that piece of property which providentially was now in our hands, a Christian community of some 150 souls settled.

After the war these peasants, of course, went back to their villages, back to their fields, and Sharan Nagar became empty again. However, as I had anticipated, now one Christian family and now another would get a job in Takhatpur, an expanding town. I arranged that they could buy plots in Sharan Nagar cheaply. It became theirs. They could build houses on it. In the course of four or five years quite a Christian community, some 20 or 30 houses, was established.

These could, of course, walk a quarter of a mile to worship at the church on the mission compound. But it seemed to me that they really ought to have a church building close to them. So I reserved the choice piece of land for a church building and on that we put up a church using funds that had been given to me by friends in America. I built a five-foot wall around it, and this became the Sharan Nagar church building. It is probably the most durable church building in the area.

The expansion of any Christian community brings with it opportunities, problems, difficulties, victories and defeats that are totally unforeseen. Nobody imagines that they could happen. Nobody could anticipate them. Nobody could prepare for them. But if the missionary is there intending to do God's will, intending to take advantage of circumstances as they arise, and to solve problems as they come along, he will find a constant succession of things to do. The missionary must not bewail his hard luck. The missionary must not weep over defeats. Unfortunate events happen, often bringing with them opportunities, and should be accepted cheerfully as part of the day's work.

Agricultural Development

I cannot close this chapter without mentioning some of the efforts we made to increase the agricultural productivity of the Satnamis who were becoming Christian. These were an intensely agricultural people. They lived for their fields. Once when visiting a village, I saw a Christian ploughing a field. He had plodded along behind a team of oxen for half a day. When I met him, he was burning up with fever. He'd been working hard with a high fever all morning driving a plough. He was exhausted but went on ploughing. His field had to be sown. These friends of ours were ardent agriculturalists. Naturally I tried in every way to help them.

Some of them kept a few goats. These gave very little milk. I wrote to west India, where a Presbyterian missionary named Goheen—whose son became president of Princeton University—had developed a fine breed of goats. These thrived in India and also gave a quart of milk a day. I bought a male goat and had it sent over by train 600 miles to Bilaspur, intending to crossbreed him with the local goats and thus improve the stock. Since the missionary's name was Goheen, I called this young goat Goheen. Unfortunately, he got worms and died despite all the medication we could give him.

Another time we tried to improve the little village chickens. These are closely related to the Indian jungle fowl, from which all the chickens in the world are descended. Village chickens weigh only a pound or two and lay only 20 very small eggs a year—two settings. White Leghorn chickens in America lay 250-300 eggs a year and weigh five pounds! We reasoned that if we could get some good White Leghorn blood into these village chickens, if we could crossbreed the village chickens with White Leghorns, the village chickens would have more and bigger eggs and much more meat.

The villagers liked the idea. Consequently, I imported eggs and set them under village hens in a pen next to our house. After 21 days, the chicks hatched. Soon we had a flock of six White Leghorn hens and four roosters. Our arrangement was that if the villagers brought in two little eggs, I'd give them one big egg. They did this with great pleasure. Soon in the homes of village Christians a little Indian hen, brown, hard to see against the ground, was clucking merrily, being followed by a dozen little white chicks. The venture was succeeding.

The idea was a good one, but, alas, it foundered on an unforeseen rock. Those white chicks were so easily seen against the ground that hawks constantly flying over Indian villages would see them, swoop down and carry them off. The hawks did not carry off the little brown Indian chicks; but they slaughtered the White Leghorns. So the venture did not prosper. A few villagers so well protected their chicks that they grew so big that a hawk could not get them. But the experiment was not nearly as successful as I had hoped.

Another time I had the opportunity to buy a half-dozen specially fine buffalo cows of a breed that gave more milk than the local buffalo cows. These were not common in our part of India but were common 600 miles north. Some entrepreneur had brought down a herd of six buffalo cows and one buffalo bull from North India. I reasoned that many of our villagers drove a team of castrated buffalo bulls. It would be a small thing to persuade them to buy a buffalo cow that gave them five or six quarts of milk a day, rich in butter fat.

I bought the six cows and one bull and kept them there on the mission compound. We had milk in great quantities. We sold it in town to the makers of sweet meats—Indian candy—but to buy and care for a buffalo cow was such a new enterprise to our villagers that none of them had the courage to buy a single cow. All of them thought, "It is something entirely beyond me. Furthermore, if my buffalo cow would happen to die, my money would be irrevocably lost."

The teaching of this incident is that while the missionary ought to be concerned with improving agriculture, he should also recognise that it is by no means an easy task. A well-known missionary some years before we arrived there had successfully introduced peanuts and sugar cane. Both grew very well. Both became profitable crops of the area. Because he brought them in, there were plenty of peasants (entirely Hindus, by the way) who made good money. Sometimes these attempts to benefit agriculture succeed, and sometimes they do not.

In 1948 I sent a young Christian of our area, a high school graduate, to a Presbyterian agricultural school in Allahabad, where he enrolled in a four-year course. By 1952 he would be graduated and maybe by that time we would be able to employ him, so that he could give his full time and attention to improving agriculture in our area.

As I have said, God works in mysterious ways. In 1952 a wealthy farmer in Illinois who belonged to the Christian Church decided to give $20,000 to the India Mission to be used for agricultural work. This was exactly what we wanted. Since the Takhatpur area had the greatest number of village Christians—working peasants—Takhatpur was where the India Mission es-

tablished the agricultural demonstration center. The young man
we had trained in Allahabad came back. He put in his time
grafting good stock onto local mango and guava trees, testing
new varieties of rice that would yield more, encouraging the
people to buy and use fertilizer and improving agriculture in
many other ways. He was of benefit both to the Christians and to
the Hindu peasants of the area.

While the primary work of the missionary is to preach the
gospel, bring men and women to salvation, and multiply
Christian churches in receptive segments of the population, it is
also his work to benefit life by medicine, education, agriculture,
leprosy work and any other means possible. The missionary
calling is a wide calling. The long-range task—discipling every
caste, every people on earth—goes steadily forward. The
missionary can often help people and should do so **provided
that the long-range goal is kept clearly in mind and
constantly worked at.**

Conclusion

I trust that this unvarnished account of how Mrs. McGavran
and I and our missionary and national colleagues tried to obey
eternal God's command to proclaim the gospel and disciple one
of the many unreached peoples of earth will be of use to new
missionaries.

Some will be Indian missionaries sent out by missionary
societies founded in India. Some will be sent out by societies in
the United States or Europe. Some will be sent out by societies
in Japan, Korea, Brazil or other nations of the world. As these
fan out all over the earth, some will go to help new young denominations—Younger Churches. They will teach in their
seminaries or day schools. They will work in their hospitals and
leprosy homes. That is certainly one task.

However, I hope that most new missionaries will be sent out
by their missionary societies to select a **responsive unreached**
ethnic unit, and engage in an enduring effort to develop a strong
people movement in that *ethnos*.

Missionaries ought to engage in **enduring** efforts to multiply
churches in specific units. **Missionary societies ought to send
out a succession of missionaries for many decades—till an
ongoing people movement to Christ results in the formation**

of hundreds of ongoing congregations and strong new denominations.

All such endeavours will be different. Each will present its own opportunities and obstacles. Each group of missionaries will do what they believe will result in vigourous, self-propagating churches in their particular population. If this account of our somewhat unsuccessful labours in the Satnami people aids or encourages these efforts, we shall thank God. Carrying out the Great Commission is a cooperative enterprise. Each missionary's achievements go toward building that new world in which "every knee shall bow and every tongue confess that Jesus Christ is Lord."

> I hope that most new missionaries will be sent out by their missionary societies to select a responsive unreached ethnic unit, and engage in an enduring effort to develop a strong people movement in that *ethnos*.

10

Effective Evangelism is Discipling a Whole People

This last chapter deals with principles and methods which underlie the propagation of the gospel, all multiplication of new churches, and all carrying out of the Great Commission in every country of the world. The Satnami story recounted in the previous nine chapters is one small illustration of these general principles. We now turn from a particular story to a theory of mission that God has blessed throughout the ages in all lands.

Multiplication of Christian congregations in every segment of the world's population—Christianisation—is the chief purpose of the missionary enterprise. Until this is recognised modern missions stand in grave danger of becoming a multitude of good activities that have very little to do with carrying out the Great Commission or with bringing multitudes of men and women to believe on Jesus Christ. Some modern missions seem quite content to let the lost remain lost while carrying out helpful activities of one sort or another. If we are to be truly Christian, this unbiblical position must be rejected. Mission must again become what it has been historically—proclaiming the gospel to all the peoples of the world (pieces of the vast mosaic of mankind) with the clear intention that they be won to fervent, believing, obedient discipleship.

This biblical understanding of the mission task helped me understand these principles that have underlain all expansion of the gospel from the Day of Pentecost onward. These principles and none others led to the evangelisation of my ancestors (and of most Americans and Europeans) in Scotland, England, Scandinavia, Germany, and France.

Today we see a rising interest in evangelising and discipling unreached peoples in every nation. Concern to do this is mounting in almost every country. For the first time we are beginning to understand that far more unreached than reached **peoples** are found in the 3 billion (rapidly becoming 4 billion) who have yet to believe. We are also understanding that discipling unreached peoples (segments of society, *jatiyan* in Hindi) is the real meaning of the Great Commission. **Effective worldwide missions are in reality just beginning.**

While the missionary enterprise has been hugely successful in some places in the world, in many others it has barely started.

In China we see examples both of very slow growth and of tremendous growth. There after more than 100 years of missions, in 1948 were only 6 million Christians, both Protestant and Roman Catholic. While there were many mission stations, the number of Christians compared to the huge population was very small indeed—perhaps 1% of the total population. Then after 1967 and after Chairman Mao's great leap backward, a tremendous multiplication of house churches took place. This occurred largely as a result of Christian radio broadcasts. Today there are at least 50 million Christians in mainland China—5% of the total population of 1 billion.

When we look at the world as a whole, the percentage of Christians in each nation-state and, indeed, in each district, county or city, varies enormously. In the Muslim world there are very few Christians—not even one-tenth of one percent. In many other countries, such as Africa south of the Sahara, the states of Kerala and Mizoram in India, and all the countries of Latin America, 20-90% of the total population has become at least nominally Christian. In Japan despite the fact that missionaries can get visas to go there easily, only one percent of the population is Christian. In short, every nation and indeed every urban or rural area presents a different stage in carrying out the Great Commission. In many, Christianisation has barely begun. In a few a majority of the population claims to be Christian.

Furthermore, we are realising that even in a country like America many segments of the population are unreached. The 6 million Jews in the United States constitute an unreached people. So do the secular French Canadians, and the highly materialistic Chicanos (25 million or more), who are considered nominally

Roman Catholic. Most of these are active materialists and secularists. Indeed, it would not be far wrong to call most of them pagans. That word "pagan" is certainly true of many of the educated white population of the United States and Europe.

In the little country of Albania, which in 1950 was 70% Muslim, 20% Greek Orthodox, and 10% Roman Catholic, the Marxist-Stalinist government has completely eradicated all traces of religion. There are no mosques, no churches, and no Christian schools. The crosses on graves have been destroyed.

The modern world is a battleground between secularism and Christianity, and sometimes secularism wins surprising victories.

God Commands the Discipling of *Ethne*

As Christian men and women see the thousands of unreached peoples in every country of the world—America, India, Europe, China and on and on—they hear Christ's command: "Disciple all the peoples—*ethne, jatiyan*—of planet earth. Enroll them as Christians. Bring them to a knowledge of me, faith in me, and obedience to me."

That is Christ's command, recorded in Matthew 28:19f. Christians are to win whole peoples, whole *ethne*, whole *jatiyan*. Let the reader in India open his Bible and turn to Matthew 28:19. In Hindi this reads *sab jatiyan ko chela karo* (disciple all the castes). Of course, winning individuals is the beginning part of winning peoples. **The Greek words are** *matheteusate* **(disciple)** *panta* **(all)** *ta ethne. Ethne* **means the ethnic units, i.e., all the peoples of the world, all the** *jatiyan* **(castes) in India and elsewhere.**

Reaching Beyond Established Churches

Missionary societies, in the West and the East, the North and the South, are now recognising that the mission task is precisely to press on beyond already established churches. It is to reach those **peoples (those** *jatiyan*, **those segments of society)** that have **not** yet been discipled.

For example, in India there are more than 3,000 castes and tribes. Among these 3,000 only 21 have experienced any major movement towards Christ. In about 50 more *jatiyan* a few hundreds or a few thousands have become Christian, but the movement has then stopped. So only within 71 of the 3,000 unreached peoples has there been any small or sizeable movement to Christ. These may be called the 71 "reached people'—*jatiyan*. **Outside of these, in the great subcontinent of India are at least 2,929 unreached peoples. Since there exist 2,929 unreached *jatiyan* in India, the main task of most denominations and missionary societies (Indian and Western) must be to press on beyond the congregations they have fathered and bring to birth new clusters of congregations among the 2,929 *jatiyan* who have yet to be discipled.**

This reaching beyond will sometimes be done by missionaries and missionary societies through the denominations already geographically near. For example, in northeast India any reaching of unreached tribes is going to be done largely by the million or more Baptists and the 200,000 Presbyterians who are already there. At present no foreigners are allowed to work there. The New Delhi government considers northeast India, lying so close to China, to be a very sensitive area, closed to foreigners.

However, in many places and many countries it will be quite possible and necessary for missionary societies (of that nation and of other nations) to press on **beyond** the national Branches of the Universal Church. The Churches on location cannot possibly evangelise the whole population. They will do very well if they disciple a tenth of it. So effectively evangelising and discipling the 90-98% that will remain will be the task of missionaries. These may come from India, North America, Korea, Japan, Africa, or Latin America. Missionaries are sent out by living churches everywhere. They go to peoples who have yet to believe. They go to the unreached peoples of the world. These unreached may be in England, Sweden, Canada, America, or some other "Western" land. Or they may be in China, Japan, Thailand, Indonesia, Zambia, or Argentina; it makes little difference.

It is important to remember that in vast populations there is no church. In the Muslim world, in Tunisia, Libya, Afghanistan, and Saudi Arabia there is no indigenous Christian church—a church of these people. Any proclamation of the gospel must be done by missionaries.

In the same way while 20% of the people of the state of Kerala in southwest India are Christians, the great Nair caste of about 5 million souls in Kerala is an unreached *jati*. It has practically no Christians. No missionaries are working to disciple it. No denomination has taken the Nair caste on its heart. Not one intends to evangelise Nairs, bring Nairs to Christ, use whatever means of presenting the gospel understandable to Nairs, and multiply churches in which Nairs are members, deacons, elders and pastors. When Nairs become Christian they ought to remain Nairs. They ought not to automatically become Harijans, Syrians or Europeans.

To be sure, all Christians hope that the time will come when men and women of all castes, all segments of population, all races, on becoming Christian will worship together. The fact remains that the world at the present time is divided into linguistic and ethnic groups. It is divided into economic and educational segments—the highly educated and the illiterate, the rural and the urban. If we would look closely at what is actually happening today in all nations, we would see that congregations are being formed in many different segments of society. This is natural. This is inevitable. This is what happened in the Roman world. One can read about it in the New Testament. Jews came to faith. Hellenists came to faith. A large number of priests came to faith. Various groups of Greeks came to faith. The Samaritans came to faith but continued as Samaritans. This will continue to happen today.

As the peoples are discipled, they will **eventually** come to think of themselves as descendants of one man Adam, and hence brothers. They will believe themselves to be equally sinners, equally saved, and hence equal in the sight of God. They are all brothers and sisters and servants of Christ.

Nevertheless, discipling unreached peoples does not mean and must not be allowed to mean bringing all the peoples of the world into those churches that have grown strong in some other segment of society. It rather means exactly what the Scriptures say. It means discipling *panta ta ethne*.

The *ethne*, the *jatiyan* will always remain. Tamil speakers will continue to speak Tamil. Japanese speakers will continue to speak Japanese. But they will be Christian Tamil speakers and Christian Japanese.

We read in Revelation 7:9 that at the end time there will be before the throne of God in heaven men from every *ethnos* and all tribes and tongues and peoples. **All these segments of society will remain until the end time.**

What must missionaries and missionary societies anticipate when they obey Christ's call in this modern world, where we find many different segments of society, many different unreached people groups?

Today the opportunity and the ability to reach these unreached peoples has mounted astronomically. We can get to them very easily in buses, lorries, trains, jet planes, and other modern means of transportation. We can spread the message to them by radio. We can print it in books and pamphlets and distribute them. We can evangelise their people who come to Europe, North America, Australia and Latin America. The opportunities for evangelism were never brighter. What must missionaries, missionary societies and, indeed, all Christians anticipate when they obey Christ's call to win the unreached peoples, the unreached *jatiyan*? They must answer three questions.

Discerning an Unreached People, a *Jati*

First, how will an unreached people appear to the national church, the missionary or his society? I mention several ways.

a. An unreached people may appear as a tribe that occupies a particular geographical area. For example, the Maasai in Kenya are a tribe and live in Maasailand. In Maasailand there are a few merchants from other tribes, but the great bulk of the people are Maasai. If a missionary goes to them, the people that he works with will be Maasai.

If he were to go to the Konyak Nagas of Nagaland, India, he would meet chiefly Konyak Nagas. If he were to go to the northwest corner of Thailand, he would be in a territory where there were only a few Thai, Sagaw Karens, Kachins or Lisu. Most of the people would be Po Karens. Or,

b. The missionary might see the one people to which God sent him as living physically intermixed with existing Christians, but totally unreached and totally separate. An example of this would be the Jews in America. Another example would be the Nairs in Kerala. They are an educated, able, well-to-do caste. They are businessmen, educators, and land owners. Nairs are a Respectable Caste. They pass by the doors of Syrian, Roman Catholic and Protestant churches every day. They vote for Christians on occasion. They live physically intermingled with Christians. But very few Nairs have become, or are becoming, Christians. Nairs are an unreached people.

There are literally tens of thousands of peoples like the Nairs. The Jews of North America live physically intermingled with Christians, but psychologically and spiritually are a great distance from them.

Moishe Rosen, the missiological genius who started the Jews for Jesus movement, says that when a Jew hears the gospel, it is meaningless to him. He doesn't say, "This is good news for me." He says, "There must be a lot of Gentiles around. I keep hearing this Gentile talk. It may have meaning for them, but it has no meaning for me."

In short, the Jew regards the gospel as an invitation to spiritual adultery. Or if he carries it further, he accounts the gospel as ethnic suicide. He cannot be a Jew and follow the Messiah. Jews for Jesus, encountering this mindset, proclaim Christ, saying, "You must and can remain a Jew while becoming a Jew for Jesus. You can worship on Saturday, not Sunday. You can circumcise your boy babies. You can totally abstain from pork. You can have a rabbi and a cantor on the platform when you worship. Ethnically you are and will remain a Jew while loving the Lord Jesus Christ and obeying Him in all matters."

So, an unreached people may appear to the missionary and his society as a people living intermingled with Christians but yet totally unreached.

c. A third example of an unreached people may be one that some missionary society is beginning to reach. The society has established a few congregations amongst the million or more souls who compose the unreached people. The gospel has been accepted by a few converts. Maybe one percent or one-tenth of one percent of this unreached people has become Christian. In short, some work is being carried on, some evangelism is being done among this unreached people. **Nevertheless, this segment of society should be regarded as unreached.**

Suppose there is a people numbering a half a million, and in it the Episcopal Church of South India has begun to work. Its **proclamation** reaches maybe 50,000, but only a couple of thousand or fewer have been baptised. That still leaves 450,000 who never hear the gospel. It also leaves nearly 500,000 who have no intention of being baptised. This is still an unreached people and will continue to be an unreached people. Until the Church of South India has won to Christ and baptised at least 50,000 and planted at least 500 churches, this people, this *jati* must be considered unreached.

Missionary Intentions

The second question is, what will the missionary intend to do when he arrives among an unreached people? Or, what will the missionary society intend by taking any one of these unreached peoples on its heart? I mention two basic intentions.

a. Both missionary and the missionary society must intend a work lasting many years. The discipling of a people is not some lark undertaken on a Saturday afternoon. It's not something concerning which you say, "We'll give this a whirl for a year or two. If it works, splendid. If it doesn't, we'll go back to the churches that sent us out."

No! As a missionary society takes an undiscipled people to its heart, it must intend many years of prayer and labour: "We hear your command, Lord Christ. We intend to proclaim the gospel and multiply churches among this people until You call us back. If this means a lifetime or the sending of a succession of missionaries for the next 50 years, we are prepared to do that. Lord Jesus, we are going there not in accordance with our own desires, but in obedience to your command, voiced so clearly in Matthew 28:19."

b. The missionary and his society should carry on evangelism which intends to begin and nurture a people movement. The goal is not merely to proclaim the gospel, though that will certainly be done. That's the beginning stage. The purpose is through the proclamation of the gospel to lead as many as possible individuals and groups of that specific people to believe on Jesus

Christ, and to lead them in such a way that a movement to Christ flourishes and extends the length and breadth of that entire segment of society. That is merely obeying the Great Commission. We are told in plain language that because all authority has been given to Jesus Christ, therefore we are to go and disciple *panta ta ethne*. We are commanded to bring *ethnos* after *ethnos* (*jati* after *jati*, tribe after tribe, segment after segment) to Christ. This necessitates people movements. In every nation-state of the world, evangelism must intend to begin and nurture the movement of whole peoples to Christ. The people is not destroyed when it becomes Christian. It is redeemed.

As missionaries proclaim the gospel, God blesses two kinds of increase in the Church. Sometimes the missionaries get one-by-one converts. Sometimes they get groups of converts, i.e., a people movement. God blesses both ways, and both ways are seen in the history of the expansion of Christianity as normal and entirely proper ways of spreading faith.

The Satnami story speaks very well to the one-by-one mode of becoming Christian. It tells of mission practice that most missions in India and other countries carried out in the 19th and 20th centuries. When the gospel is proclaimed anywhere, men and women respond in two ways. Either they become Christians one by one or by movements of large numbers of interconnected families. Let us look first at the one-by-one mode.

As the gospel was proclaimed, a few individuals now and then would believe in Jesus Christ and become His open followers. In India this always resulted in their being outcasted, impoverished, and left without any means of support. As a result, all over India the most common way Christian communities were started was to help believers maintain life. This usually meant some form of economic assistance— employment, grain loans, money loans, assistance in starting a new livelihood, and on and on.

On the other hand, the movement of a people—a *jati* or caste—to Christ began as groups of people became Christian. These received no material help at all. This was necessary both theologically and financially. It had to be very clearly said that becoming a Christian did not mean financial assistance. Our Lord said to the rich young ruler, "Sell all you have and give it to the poor. Then come and follow me." He sent out His twelve apostles with very scanty equipment. All successful movements to Christ have followed this "no financial aid policy."

All missionaries realized this and, indeed, accepted it as their long-term principle of action. However, when as a result of preaching the gospel someone believed and was immediately deprived of all means of sustenance, missionaries of all denominations in all parts of India and other parts of the world also helped converts stay alive. They would give them financial aid of one sort and another. They might employ them. The best of them might become teachers of the Word. Those with land might be aided to remain on it. All were told repeatedly that no one receives money for becoming a Christian and were encouraged to become financially independent as soon as possible.

As world evangelisation continues in the post-imperial age, the pattern of all effective missionaries is increasingly pattern two. They enroll as new Christians only those who can live the Christian life without becoming dependent on the missionary. Indeed, one may confidently state that the great movements to Christ in all lands occur only as people movements that are not aided financially in any way take place. Becoming a Christian then appears to all not as a way of getting out of financial difficulties but as a way of life enormously superior to whatever religion the convert is leaving, be that idol worship or demon worship or secularism.

The Satnami story should be read and studied as a truthful account of what many missionaries in many lands were doing. As they faced the situation where anyone becoming a Christian was immediately outcasted and had his livelihood snatched away from him, the missionaries worked out a system that enabled congregations of believers to arise. That financial help was given to some members of these small congregations led enemies of the gospel to proclaim that becoming a Christian has some financial benefits. Missiologists who see the total situation and are aware of the great sweep of history will, however, perceive that this regrettable handicap could not be avoided. Only as this is perceived as a missionary method followed by missionaries of societies in most of the districts of India, and of other nations also, will the problem be seen in its true dimensions.

It is easy in the closing decades of the 20th century to decry this procedure as wrong and to declare that no intelligent missionary would have voiced it. It is easy and wrong to say this. Devoted Christian missionaries working in all fifteen of the major language areas of India—and many other parts of the world also—found that they had just two openings before them. Either they won no Christians at all and founded no churches, or they won Christians one by one who often had to be helped economically. Thus they often established non-growing and often small congregations. Their members spoke the language naturally, they had many unconverted relatives, they were citizens of the land, they formed truly indigenous and good churches, but they were very slow growing.

Furthermore, in caste after caste God did use these one-by-one congregations to start a Christward movement that received no financial assistance. These movements spread rapidly throughout various segments of the population. It is only as Christian churches are multiplied—which, like the churches in Philippi, Corinth, and Rome, become part of the evangelising community and have no financial dependence upon their founders—that effective evangelism, discipling *ethnos* after *ethnos*, really occurs.

We hope that this book will illumine a chapter in world evangelisation. It describes an attempt to start a people movement, a castewise movement to Christ, whose members received no financial assistance at all. It hoped to start congregations that paid their pastors.

However, the resolute action of the Satnami leaders outcasting every man or woman who became a Christian, and Mahatma Gandhi's nationwide drive to hold the Untouchables in the Hindu fold, prevented the start of a successful castewise movement to Christ. A church of 10,000 converts was never established. As a result, the Satnami story tells of what missionaries of all denominations were commonly facing in India and other lands. The Satnami story tells of individual converts and small groups of four or five families who were helped in many ways. They received free education for their children. They received medical treatment in mission hospitals. They received loans on the security of gold earrings, silver bangles, or brass cooking vessels.

The first step in missions described in this book must be seen as a beginning step that often has to be taken in discipling any *ethnos*. This Satnami story is the story of a dangerous first step. It might have succeeded, but it did not. Unless this is seen, in many *ethne* a Christian movement will not begin.

In nations where the population is strongly segmented, "one-by-one from many segments," results in very small growth of a few congregations. These are most likely to become heavily dependent on the missionary. The missionary, despite every effort to avoid undue influence, finds all converts turning to him. After all, in the beginning, converts have no one else to turn to. He is the person who proclaims Christ. In the one-by-one approach the danger of the missionary having undue influence in cultural and economic matters is great.

In sharp contrast to one-by-one conversions, when men turn to Christ in a series of interrelated groups, a people movement to Christ begins in some one segment of society and flows through it. **All major advances of the Church in history, outside of already Christianised lands, have been by people movements.** As one reads the accounts in Kenneth Scott Latourette's seven-volume *History of the Expansion of Christianity*, he sees people movements again and again. There were people movements in Gaul, Great Britian, Ireland, Armenia, Russia, North Africa, and on and on. The great advances of the Church on new ground have been by people movements.

However, the earliest beginnings of a people movement are often one by one. People movements arise by the action of the Holy Spirit. They arise as first individuals and then a series of groups of one people open to the moving of the Holy Spirit. Since group movements seldom happen in the first stage of evangelism in any nation-state, one-by-one from several peoples is likely to be seen at the beginning. The missionary society and its missionaries—**whether sent out by Indian, Korean, Nigerian or Western societies makes no difference**—will therefore aim at, pray for and work for people movements to Christ. Each congregation or missionary will work for a people movement to Christ. Each will ask God to bring about the movement of an *ethnos*—a *jati*—a segment of mankind.

All congregations and missionaries will also gratefully accept and nurture all one-by-one converts. Because they are praying and working for a people movement, they will not foolishly reject one-by-one converts. They will accept them. But they will say, "Lord, make this single convert the reason why first one group and then another and then a whole series of groups from within this convert's segment of society will come to Christ. We are here, Lord, by your command, to disciple this whole people. We do not know why just one person has resolved to accept You; but we accept him, Lord, as Your precious gift. We pray that through him, his relatives, his friends and his intimates, many of his people will follow You."

Every *Ethnos* is Unique

We now turn to the third question, What must congregations, denominations, missionaries and missionary societies anticipate when they obey Christ's command to disciple *panta ta ethne*?

They must anticipate that the one people to which God sends them will be different from all others.

This book is the story of an effort to disciple the Satnami segment of Indian society. What has been told in the preceding chapters is not reproducible point for point in any other *jati* in India or segment of society in another nation. Every people stands at a different place in history. Frequently it has a different language. Almost always it has a different economic base. It has different social customs, it has a different culture. It is itself quite distinct.

For example, there was a Muslim people movement in central and east Java starting about 1965 and continuing on to the present day, by which 100,000 and maybe by this time 200,000 Muslims have become Christians. Evangelisation (church multiplication) in that country among that people is very different from evangelisation among Muslims in Egypt, London or Detroit. And that in turn is quite different from winning Muslims in Bangladesh.

Planting churches among one segment of Chinese people (the highly educated Chinese in West Malaysia) is again different from any of these other instances I have mentioned. The missionary must realise that the people to which God sends him is quite different from other peoples in the world. Yet there are striking similarities! The account in this book of an attempt to disciple the Satnamis will, I hope, cast much light on mission work among many unreached peoples.

This Book and Nine Principles

This book presents one people, the Satnamis, and tells of an 18-year effort by one missionary family to preach the gospel to them and to start a people movement among them.

The Satnamis were not physically unreached. They did not live beyond unpassable swamps or uncrossable mountains. They had, as a matter of fact, heard the gospel from five different missions for many years before this missionary got there. Each mission had won several hundred converts. Most had remained Christians; some had reverted to Satnamism. There were in 1936, when this attempt began, all told in five different denominations about 15,000 who said, "Our fathers, grandfathers, or great grandfathers were Satnamis. We are now Christians, but our ancestors were of that segment of society."

Had anyone spoken to the still Hindu Satnamis, they would have said, "Yes, we have been hearing this gospel for a long time. A few of our people have been deceived, have become Christians, and ruined their caste. We won't give our girls to them in marriage any more. We won't eat with them. They're now a separate caste—Christians. Perhaps it's been good for them to become Christians, but it's nothing that we Satnamis as a whole are going to do. We are not going to ruin our caste."

This instant, uncompromising outcasting of any who become Christian is one of the striking similarities in discipling the ethnic units of mankind. In most other pieces of the human mosaic, becoming a Christian (especially if the step is taken alone) means suffering outcasting or some less painful degree of exclusion. That was the situation.

Between 1860 and 1936 out of a population of about a half a million Satnamis perhaps 3,000 had left Satnamism to become Christians in five Protestant denominations. These converts with their children and grandchildren in 1936 numbered about 15,000. These lived in small groups in or near the 20 or more mission stations in the *tahasils* and districts of the plain of Chattisgarh. This measured 150 by 200 miles (see maps).

A merit of this case study is its factuality, its careful description of the many opportunities that across the 18 years faced the missionary and his Indian colleagues, the many attempts made to meet these opportunities, to plough these fields, sow these seeds and reap these harvests. It is an account of some victories, as men and women were won to Christ and organised into ongoing churches. It is also an account of many defeats, where evangelism did not win anybody or where a group was won and then reverted to idolatry. This is a real story of a real missionary facing real conditions. It gives an accurate picture of what reaching a people for Christ is likely to mean in any part of India and, indeed, other nations.

As soon as we say this, however, we must recall that each people is different, so that exactly this will not be reproduced in the heart of China or in the highlands of Afghanistan, a city in Europe or America, or other castes or language areas in India. Readers may be sure that as they obey Christ in other segments of humanity, urban and rural, educated and uneducated, in India, China, Africa, Latin America and the United States, **exactly these incidents** will not occur. **The following nine principles, however, will be widely applicable.** We may confidently expect most of them to occur again and again in most segments of society if these are evangelised **effectively**.

Nine Universal Principles

Since any serious attempt to disciple a segment of society, an *ethnos* or *jati*, involves a missionary society, a missionary, his assistants and national colleagues, and others, in recounting the nine principles we shall frequently use all four terms interchangeably. Each member of the team plays his part. In some cases the missionary plays the leading part. In others his assistants, colleagues or the national church do that.

The first principle is that from among the many segments of society in any geographical area the missionary must **choose one that appears to be most ready, most likely to turn to salvation**. Since the missionary does not know which of the many segments of society will prove most receptive, his work for the first few months or even years will be to learn the

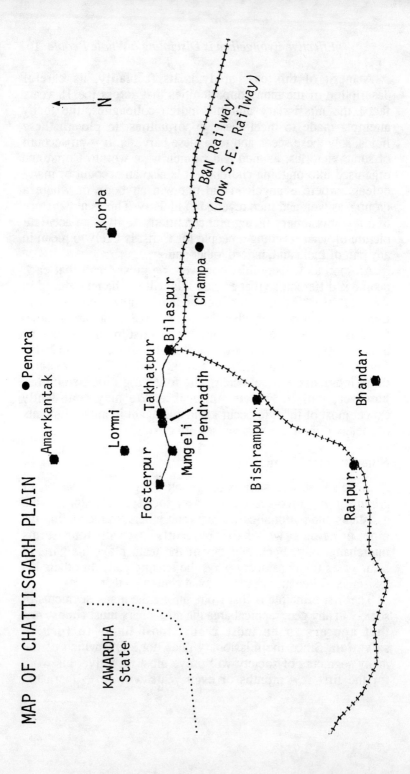

MAP OF CHATTISGARH PLAIN

different segments of the population. He will ask himself, What are the *ethne* in this rural district or urban area? How many segments are there? Which ones appear most resistant? Which appear most responsive? Among which are congregations likely to multiply?

The missionary may find that in the rural district or organisation where he is working there is a segment of population that in a neighbouring district has become largely Christian. He will at once conclude that this is the *ethnos* to which God has sent him. He may find that into his district have moved Christians of a given *jati* or segment of society. These are living as part of their unconverted *jati* or segment of society already resident in that district.

Failing these desirable indications of receptivity, he will proclaim the gospel broadly to all who will listen. Judging from the response he will then determine that this segment or this *ethnos* will be responsive. He will say, "In this *ethnos* or this particular part of the population I believe God will multiply congregations of believers."

The period of exploration, of determining the responsive segment, will probably take several—perhaps many—years.

The Church and the missionary society concerned with carrying out the Great Commission in that district should clearly realise that **the purpose of their exploratory work, their first years there, must be the finding of that people, that segment of society, that tribe or that *jati* which God has prepared to follow Christ and to which God Himself has sent them.**

The second principle is that the missionary society and its workers will **consciously adopt an *ethnos*, a *jati*, a segment of society, purposing to disciple it—that is, win it to Christian faith.** They will not simply go into an area. They will not say, "We have now gone to Tamil Nadu." "We are now at work in the great city of Dacca." These are almost meaningless generalities. They delay discipling. Instead they will pray: "O Lord our God, we have resolved to disciple this people—this *ethnos*, this *jati*—in Tamil Nadu or Cairo in Egypt or Sao Paulo in Brazil. This is our people to which You have sent us, and our lives are bound up with its members. It is our purpose to win men and women of this *jati* or segment of society to Christ. If Christ will permit it, we shall be apostles to this people, this *jati*, as Patrick was an apostle to the Irish tribes, as he led all of them to You. So Lord Jesus, make us Your apostles. Send us to this people and help us to disciple it. Lay this people—this *ethnos*—on our hearts. If it is won, we shall rejoice; if it is lost, we shall weep."

The third principle is they will then **learn that people.** A whole chapter of this book is devoted to the Satnamis, their customs and beliefs, how they arose, and where they are going. Discovering these things is the learning process. Not only must the missionary go physically to be with such-and-such a people; he must also learn that people—where did it come from, what are its antecedents, how do its members earn a living, what are their beliefs, what do they cherish, what do they hate? He will learn their language. It may be a dialect of some standard language. It may be a language of its own. He will learn its religion and culture. That is an essential step in discipling an *ethnos*.

The fourth principle is that the mission worker will **love and serve that people.** To him it is not "those people over there." It is not just an unreached people. It is my people, and I know and love its members. I will serve them in any way I can. I will constantly pray for them and their salvation. I will beseech God for certain individuals and for the salvation of the whole people. When they are oppressed, I will champion them and seek to remove their oppression. I will fight for them. I will lift them up. I will heal their diseases. I will feed their hungry. The gospel must be presented in terms that all this people, this minority, can easily understand. These are my brothers and sisters.

The fifth principle is that mission workers will always **proclaim the gospel so that it may be understood by that *ethnos*, that *jati*.** Workers will advocate the gospel in terms that will appeal to these souls. They will tell the story in a way convincing to this particular people. A proclamation of the gospel that would be convincing to hard-core Communists in Kerala would not be convincing to an aboriginal tribe living in the mountains of northeast India. The gospel must be presented to each caste, tribe or segment of society, so that accepting Christ looks good to its members. To the men and women of an unreached people that the missionary and the mission adopt, that they love and serve and champion, the gospel must be presented in terms that **they** can understand.

The sixth principle is that the missionaries **bend every effort to multiply sound, biblical congregations in the chosen *ethnos*.** The missionaries will be tempted after the first few hundreds or thousands become Christian to spend all their time in consolidating the gains. They will say, "These people know so little of the Word and are, compared to those who have been Christians for generations, so weak that the most urgent task is to see that they become good biblical Christians. Training pastors for their churches is our most urgent task. Only after these become good Christians, will they be able to lead others to Christ. These must become far better Christians before it is wise for us to seek more converts."

In sharp distinction to this common way of thinking, **any perfecting that excludes or minimizes continuous winning others to Christ is a mistake.** We must consolidate, to be sure, but we must always consolidate on the run. We must make sure that the stream of new converts never dries up, because the new converts are the growing edge of the church. If one takes a thousand Christians, stops baptising and instructs the thousand for 20 years and then expects them to win their surrounding relatives and friends, he will meet with grave disappointment. By that time they will have become a separate people. They will have few friends among their former intimates. It is essential to keep the stream of new converts flowing. The double task is, by feeding new Christians on the Word, to develop genuine Spirit-filled churches among them **and** at the same time to keep proclaiming the gospel, winning new groups to Christ, and multiplying new churches.

The seventh principle is that the missionaries **feed the new churches on the Word of God.** When people become Christians, when they believe the gospel and follow Christ, unless they are fed on the Word of God, they are likely to become very weak. They need the bread of life. They should learn the sacred accounts of the life of Christ. They ought to hear repeatedly what the Epistles say. Gradually they will come to know the Old Testament and God's provision for His people throughout the centuries.

The multiplication of churches in a responsive segment of society is not a brief task. It is a long process. It takes years to create in the hearts of men and women a belief that they are truly members of the body of Christ. Loyalty to the church and habits of worship and giving develop slowly, more slowly in some *ethne* and more rapidly in others. The church ought soon to become self-supporting and self-governing. And perhaps more than anything else, the Christians themselves, filled with the Holy Spirit and illumined by the Word of God, should propagate the gospel. All this takes continual feeding of new Christians on the Word of God.

The eighth principle is that the missionaries ought to **rejoice with those who rejoice and weep with those who weep.** The missionary task is not only a task of glorious endeavour going from one height to another. The missionary, whether a national or a foreigner, must also tread the dark, dangerous canyons and sometimes go through the valley of the shadow of death. He will be present as the new Christians meet difficulties both external and internal. He must be there to help them surmount temptation and attack, and come out victorious.

The ninth principle is to **hold the discipling of that *ethnos* steadily in mind year after year.** If the missionary scatters his efforts and after establishing two or three churches in one *jati* turns to some other people and plants a church and then goes on to a third people and evangelises there, he will likely win no *ethnos* to Christ. If the missionary, after establishing a few churches, turns to medicine, education, development, famine relief, pastoral training or the like, he will soon find that he is spending nine-tenths of his time and money on good works and one-tenth or even less on multiplying new congregations in the *ethnos* to which God has sent him. Discipling the *ethnos* will not go forward. But if the two or three churches won this year are followed by more and more churches planted in the same people in the following years, **then** the chances of his discipling that particular *ethnos* are bright. Pastors and missionaries should bend every effort to multiply sound biblical churches in each segment of society to which God has sent them.

Effective Christians must keep on working, especially when the going is hard. Discipling or enrolling a segment of mankind into Christ's Church usually means a work lasting 20, 50 or 100 years. During that time there will be many difficulties and many dangers. There will be sickness. There will be opposition. There will be ridicule. There will be death. As this case study of the attempted evangelisation of the Satnamis has been read, the reader has seen these difficulties, defeats and persecutions again and again. They are part of effective evangelism. Much of the New Testament was written by a missionary facing difficulty after difficulty. For many years he was **in prison**. All the apostles, we are told, died martyrs deaths. The missionary, or indeed the lay evangelist or other messenger of God, lays his hand to the plough, resolved not to turn back. When his plough breaks and he has to go to his house to make a new one, he returns to the field. He is one of God's warriors, and he intends to go on fighting despite the wounds. Ignatius Loyola's prayer needs to be written on the heart of every missionary. "Grant, O Lord, that I may serve Thee without flinching, love thee without reserve, fight on without heeding the wounds, and labour asking for no reward save that of knowing that I do Thy will."

People Movement Approach Summarised

As we look back over these nine principles in the light of the whole Satnami story, we can now say a few words in summary concerning the people movement approach. In the enormously complex mosaic of mankind each people movement will, of course, be somewhat different from all others. Yet a certain sameness is also observable.

We must always remember that mission goes forward under the express command of the ultimate Authority in the universe. He to whom all authority in heaven and earth has been given (Matthew 28:18) commands His Church, saying, "*Matheteusate panta ta ethne.*" This command is given to the entire Body of Christ, to the whole Body and all its members.

But to any one Branch of the Universal Church, to any one mission and sometimes to any one Christian leader or pastor or missionary, the command is different. One man or small group of men cannot possibly disciple *panta ta ethne,* all the ethnic units in the world. The Lord Christ commands one person, or one group of Christians to disciple one single *ethnos*. This truth is often obscured by the fact that missionaries are sent, not to an *ethnos*, but to a country. Missionaries say, "We are going to

Zambia, Argentina, Japan or Pakistan." This, of course, is true.
But none of them can possibly evangelise the whole country
they have just mentioned. All missionaries should therefore see
their real work as discipling one *ethnos* or more. Most of the
great advances of the Christian faith have taken place as
unbelieving *ethnos* after *ethnos* turned to Christ. The great
Gregory the Illuminator around A.D. 300 went to his *ethnos*, the
Armenians, and during his lifetime won them all to Christ. The
great Patrick went to Ireland in the year A.D. 420 and in the next
40 years won 127 Irish tribes to Christian faith. All across Africa
south of the Sahara the Christian faith advances as tribe after
tribe becomes substantially Christian. For example, despite a
hundred years' work by missionaries of the Church of Scotland
and the English Methodists, the Ibibio in southeast Nigeria were
largely pagan until after World War II, when a great movement
to Christ started among them.

A Nigerian police sergeant about 1948 became a believing,
Spirit-filled Christian. He received from a sister of Eva Braun,
Hitler's mistress, a Bible correspondence course published by
the Churches of Christ in Nashville, Tennessee. He was studying
the Bible course and, impelled by the Holy Spirit, he was used
by God to start a people movement among the Ibibios. Churches
of Christ missionaries from America assisted him. The baptised
believers in 1988 number about 90,000, or a total Christian
community of about 180,000. In addition the movement has
spread to other parts of Nigeria. Some authorities say that there
are another 90,000 baptised believers meeting in Churches of
Christ in other parts of Nigeria.

In 1931 as Russell Morse, who had been sent by the United
Christian Missionary Society to Batang, on the eastern edge of
Tibet, and had lived there for some years seeking to win
Tibetans to Christ, was coming back to the United States on
furlough, a strange thing happened. Since the Japanese
controlled the eastern China route out of Batang, Morse turned
south and west. He crossed several high ranges and plunged
down into deep valleys as he made his way out into India. In one
of the deep valleys, partly in China and partly in north Burma,
he met the *ethnos* to which God had sent him. This was the Lisu
tribe. They were delighted with his message. They begged him

to stay. He told them he would return, and proceeded on into India.

Immediately after his furlough he did return. In the depth of the Depression, the United Christian Missionary Society would not open a new field, so he raised support from many congregations and went back as an independent missionary. Sixty years later there are now over 100,000 Lisu who are Christian. Russell Morse obeyed a command to disciple one receptive *ethnos*, the Lisu.

Between 1968 and 1978 missionaries of the Gospel Missionary Union working in high Ecuador found a receptive Quechua tribe. There are over 50 tribes of Quechuas living in the high Andes. The one in which the Gospel Missionary Union worked had been quite resistant. For more than 60 years its members had considered that becoming a biblical Christian was a work of the devil. Missionaries and their few converts were frequently beaten, assaulted, and ridiculed. No decent Quechua would become a biblical Christian.

Then in 1968 a people movement began in that one particular tribe in Chimborazo province. In 1968 after 66 years of work there were only 315 baptised believers. "By 1972, the baptised numbered 2,356" and by 1976 there were 10,027 baptised believers. The total Christian community including children numbered at least 25,000 ("Quechuas on the March in Ecuador" by Gunter Schulze in *Church Growth Bulletin*, Vol. XII, No. 5, May 1976, pp. 529-531). An unstoppable people movement had developed. This movement in the late 1970's and 1980's spread to others of the more than 50 Quechua tribes.

In May 1987 Don Palmer of the headquarters staff of the Gospel Missionary Union wrote the following:

Quechua churches now number 405
Quechua baptised members—37,000
Quechua church adherents—92,000
Theological Education by Extension—40 centers
  with 460 students
Bible Institute—105 students
Radio stations—2 owned and operated by Quechua
  believers
Film showings—450 with an audience of 81,000
  during 1986

> Translation—Old Testament completed, the New Testament revised; the entire Bible to be printed soon. . . .
>
> Quechua Christians from Chimborazo province have founded at least 25 churches in Colombia and Venezuela, most of these by believers from the San Antonio church, made up of a great number of Quechuas who are traveling merchants. They evangelize and form groups wherever they go. And the Quechuas in Ecuador itself have started a number of fairly good sized churches in some of the major cities such as Guayaquil [on the coast] and Quito [on the highlands]. They have also sent missionaries to evangelise Quechuas in another area of Ecuador where there are very few evangelicals among them at this point.[9]

Accounts of people movements similar to these could be written for *ethne* (peoples) from many parts of the world. Successful people movements are, of course, far outnumbered by unsuccessful ones. Sometimes the movement of a people is mishandled by their national leaders or by the missionaries. Sometimes the opposition is too fierce. Sometimes wars stop a movement.

However, as the gospel is preached throughout the entire world, the Church of Jesus Christ grows chiefly by people movements. One-by-one accessions from the world do occur, but they seldom result in great growth. Movements of peoples, however, when they are successful bring tremendous increase in the church.

As small bands of Christians of all nationalities carry out the Great Commission, as they are revived by the Holy Spirit and renew their dedication, each band works steadily forward multiplying biblical churches in its segment of society.

Conclusion

We hope this book will help missionaries, missionary societies, denominations, pastors and committed Christians to adopt, love, serve and disciple at least one unreached *ethnos*, one

---

[9] Don Palmer letter to Donald McGavran, May 15, 1987.

segment of mankind. We hope it will encourage missionaries in difficulties. These may be missionaries of any race—Asians, Africans, Europeans, or Americans. They may have been born in any continent. We hope this book will set their feet on the right paths, and help them see God's will for their lives in the midst of tens of thousands of unreached peoples. As missionaries from India and many other lands in the years ahead hear men from many a Macedonia pleading, "Come over and help us," we hope they will at once go to Macedonia.

We also trust that this story of a particular effort among the Satnami people between the years 1936 and 1954 will help all workers become effective propagators of the gospel. We pray that God will bless the efforts to win *panta ta ethne* to Christian faith. Our Lord has commanded it—*matheteusate panta ta ethne*—in English, "disciple all the pieces of the vast human mosaic'; in Hindi, *sab jatiyan ko chela karo*. We are certain that the Lord will help all missionary-minded men and women become effective propagators of the gospel.

"All authority in heaven and on earth has been given to me. Therefore *matheteusate panta ta ethne*"—multiply biblical congregations in all segments of society at home and abroad.

Index

DATE DUE
